About the Author

Gail has both personal and professional experience in disability. After working with people with disabilities for many years she became a mother for the second time to Lachlan, who has autism. Gail continues to work and study in this area (Social Science, Welfare and Education in Disabilities) and lives with her family in Sydney.

Dedication

To our dear friend Linda, Righteous Pups Australia and
our family and friends

Gail Simpkins

PRAYING FOR STRAWBERRIES

AUSTIN MACAULEY PUBLISHERS™

LONDON • CAMBRIDGE • NEW YORK • SHARJAH

A CIP catalogue record for this title is available from the British Library.

ISBN 978-1-78693-873-2 (Paperback)
ISBN 978-1-78693-874-9 (E-Book)
www.austinmacauley.com

First Published (2017)
Austin Macauley Publishers Ltd.™
25 Canada Square
Canary Wharf
London
E14 5LQ

Acknowledgments

Thanks to Lachlan for noticing what others often miss and for showing us unique ways of doing things and to Itsal for assisting us all each day and reminding us when we become too busy to remember. We could not be more proud of you both.

I am so grateful to Professor Trevor R Parmenter for your writing and encouragement along the way which motivated me to go ahead and finish this project; but most of all thank you for being a much-needed voice for people with a disability and their families. Thank you for everything you do.

Thanks to Joanne Baker, Jenny Atkins, Kelly Stevens and the rest of team at Righteous Pups Australia as well as their sponsors, for training Itsal and showing us how to give Lachlan back much of his independence. Your dedication to make a difference is amazing and you have made a huge difference to us.

Thanks to Ross Bruzzese, a family friend of many years for your input and positive feedback, not to mention fantastic editing and writing skills. Some edits you sent late at night so I can assume you had at least a few late nights reading and editing when you were already busy enough. Thanks Ross, you are appreciated.

Thank you to Author, Jan Daisley for your mentoring time and support, and for answering my many questions along the way. You are an inspiration.

Thanks to Jo-Ann my friend/sister in law/shopping and lunch partner for your backing and positive feedback along the way and for telling me the diary was a great idea.

Thank you to my talented sister Jackie for your lovely artwork and assistance and my adorable nephew Billy for your IT skills and help.

A big thank you to photographer Treena Cousins for chasing us around the beach and capturing the most beautiful photos.

Last but not least a huge thanks to My Choice Matters on behalf of Lachlan for funding and assisting with this project.

Foreword

It has been a privilege to walk beside Gail and Lachlan throughout the year as each month's diary appeared. What a joy to witness how the true diversity of the human condition has unfolded, showing that difference can be respected, treasured and valued, rather than being seen so often from a negative perspective. A person with autism challenges the way we perceive difference.

Despite his struggle with verbal communication, Lachlan has demonstrated how he feels, what makes him happy, and what makes him sad or fearful. These are normal human experiences, but so often we never venture behind some of the traits that superficially identify someone as being different, and hence we fail to see a real person.

Gail's diary opens a window that allows us to appreciate the humanness of Lachlan who brings joy (and sometimes tears) to his family, not at all dissimilar to other families' experiences.

It is usually mothers who bear much of the responsibility for caring for a family member with a disability. Gail's diary reveals a combination of fragility and resilience that many mothers in similar circumstances demonstrate. It is hard to imagine how constant are the concerns when your child may be at risk as they navigate the barriers and challenges thrown up by a perceived impairment of mind or body.

There are so many treasured experiences that Gail and Lachlan have shared with us; some poignant, but most uplifting, highlighting the joys of the human experience.

And what does the relationship between Itsal, Lachlan and Gail tell us about the potential of a species that is almost human in its caring and concern for its owner?

Praying for Strawberries is a remarkable story of the daily, real-life events of a mother, a child and a family who have been blessed as they travel with each other on a journey where each day unfolds with many surprises not planned for. It is this uncertainty that can be both exhilarating and challenging. The reader will not remain untouched.

Trevor R Parmenter AM
Professor Emeritus
Sydney Medical School
University of Sydney

Preface

Lachlan is usually a happy boy so I try very hard not to be sad about him having autism. After all, he does not really seem to mind. He is just happy being himself and enjoying his life, so why should I be sad about it. One of the reasons that I kept this diary was as a way to explain to our family and friends that we can still enjoy life while raising a child with autism. I also wanted to remind myself of all the positive changes Lachlan has experienced within the year which has been a constant reminder that things can and do change especially since having Itsal who is Lachlan's Autism Assistance Dog.

As Lachlan's family, we have learnt to accept Lachlan's disability and idiosyncrasies some time ago. He brings a lot of joy to those around him and we prefer to focus on this. The support of some very special family members and friends helps greatly as well as a lot of prayers. Apart from these, a sense of humour is a good thing so I'd like to share some of the funny experiences I've had being a parent of a child with autism. Not that I am laughing at my son or his disability, but I can see the differences in the way he experiences life and the world, and cannot help but see the funny side of those differences in interpretation.

Lachlan also has some unusual talents which his family know only too well and are amazed by, and as you read this diary you will see how he uses them.

Recently, since having an Autism Assistance Dog through Righteous Pups Australia named Itsal, Lachlan and his family have been able to have some wonderful new experiences for the first time. I wanted to share these with Righteous Pups, our family and friends and anyone else who may be interested.

Being a parent of a child with autism can be hard at times. Apart from the workload, we have been very limited in social participation as Lachlan has found many activities overwhelming in the past. Since Itsal's arrival we can see many things changing for the better.

In this diary, I share some daily ups and downs and Lachlan's perspective on life as well as the positive changes past and present as Lachlan learns and grows. Through trial and error Lachlan lets us know what works for him and this also changes as he grows older. Many days are an adventure.

The names of some people and places have been changed to protect privacy.

December 2014

Recently a friend asked me how Lachlan (being non-verbal) was able to communicate what he would like for Christmas. Each Christmas Lachlan looks at brochures from toy shops and department stores and points out the things he would like to ask Santa for. We cut out the pictures and stick them onto a page, along with a short letter to Santa. Next, we visit Santa and Lachlan sits beside him (not on his lap), and I read out the letter while Lachlan watches closely, making sure I do not make any mistakes. He would be quick to let me know if I made a mistake by pointing and vocalising. He would get his message across, no problem there.

This year Lachlan did not have his photo taken with Santa as we had been looking for an opportunity when there were fewer children visiting Santa so that Lachlan would feel more comfortable as he prefers fewer people and less noise to make him feel calmer about the whole Santa experience. He is a little frightened of Santa (like many children), and has not been keen to sit on his lap in the past. However, he is interested in asking him for presents so this time we wrote a letter to Santa and Lachlan posted it.

Lachlan loves Christmas and was very excited. He enjoys seeing Santa on television as he prefers not to get too close.

Each Christmas Lachlan likes to open just one present at a time and play with it. It often takes most of Christmas day for him to open his presents as he likes to get used to one new thing before opening the next present. He usually looks for presents which he suspects may be DVDs and opens those ones first. If the present he opens is a DVD he will watch it on his DVD player for a period of time, perhaps half an hour or more before moving onto other presents. He is not in a hurry to open the rest of the presents. He likes to take his time.

This year he got a new bike which Santa had left in the garage. Lachlan seemed satisfied playing with his new DVDs and other things, so the next day we showed him the bike. He seemed to like it, but only when he rides it at the park will we really know.

When Lachlan was younger each Christmas he would open his presents and if there was one he felt wary about he would put it into his toy box and not allow anyone to touch it until he became familiar with it. Sometimes this took a few days, and sometimes it took a few weeks. It was a bit like a quarantine period because after a few weeks he would begin to play with the new toy. Lachlan has always been wary of talking toys so some toys never get through quarantine. There is a toy in quarantine at the moment (a talking pig) which has been in there for a few months, so maybe she will not be joining the rest of us at all.

Chapter 1
January 2015

Saturday 10/01/15 School holidays

This morning when I heard Lachlan was awake I said "Hi," and took in his DVD player which he likes first thing in the morning. On receiving the DVD player Lachlan signed "Finish" which meant he wanted to finish me, for me to go away, leave him alone or come back later. This was usual for him as he wanted some alone time to watch his DVD. Fair enough, I thought.

Lachlan likes to play the start of the DVD over and over and I am usually pleased when he comes out of his room to change it as hearing the same part of the DVD over and over could be used as a form of 'torture' I am sure! However, this makes us, his family, more tolerant. This is one of Lachlan's repetitive behaviours associated with autism and we do have to put some limits on it, but we allow it first thing in the mornings.

Lachlan was happy for a while playing his DVDs and asked by way of a gesture (pointing to his bed) for Itsal to join him on the bed, as is usual on school days when Itsal helps to get him out of bed and get ready for school each morning.

Lachlan still wanted this to happen even though today was not a school day. Itsal happily joined Lachlan on his bed and sat on his pillow which meant Lachlan could not lie down and go back to sleep. It is totally adorable to watch as well as totally incredible. Itsal has never been instructed to lie on Lachlan's pillow. He just seems to know what will work!

It is amazing to me that Itsal knows how to do this and it works very well for all of us especially on school days. Lachlan and Itsal do not seem to want to do it differently even though it is school holiday time and Itsal does not need to wake him. They are used to the routine the way it is and they like it that way.

Lachlan ate his toast with jam for breakfast after drinking one whole bottle (750ml of juice diluted with water). He must drink the juice first and he will not eat anything before he has drunk all of the juice. He likes to do one thing at a time and for me, this makes it easier to keep track of his eating and drinking.

Lachlan looked in his picture exchange communication folder and pointed to the library picture which indicated where he wanted to go this morning. He sorted through the DVDs to be taken back, which he had borrowed on his previous visit. He has over one hundred and eighty DVDs in his collection which he has placed into five rows. After he checked all the DVDs were in their cases, he was ready to return them to the library.

At the library Lachlan picked three more DVDs to borrow. He also likes buying them as well, but he is just as happy borrowing from the library which works out well, as after a while he becomes bored watching the same ones. He has quite a collection of them in the lounge room and he does not like them to be inside the cupboard, so they stay on the outside of the cupboard because he likes to see that they are all there and in the right order.

After the library, we went to a fast food restaurant as part of Lachlan's therapy (as suggested by Debbie Alvarez, who is his speech therapist working on food issues). Debbie suggested Lachlan try eating fries which he is not willing to do yet. I wondered if he was the only child in Sydney who did not like fries. With Lachlan, we are happy for him to eat or try anything at all, as this is the only way for him to expand the variety of foods he eats. Lollies, junk food or any food at all is helpful.

Lachlan is not usually interested in most foods, even junk food does not interest him or trying new foods for that matter. Debbie says that from fries, Lachlan can progress to other sorts of hot chips and then other types of hot food. The first step towards this goal is to get Lachlan touching the fries. Debbie has suggested that after a fun play session at the fast food restaurant, buying the fries on the way out in the hope that Lachlan forms a positive association with the fries. The next step is to place them on the back seat of the car and ask him to hand them to us, one at a time.

The idea is that he will get used to touching them, and might one day want to eat one, if we are lucky, very lucky. This has happened before with other foods. On the way home Lachlan handed us a few of the fries before he decided that he could give us the whole bag of fries instead of having to touch each one. This made sense as Lachlan really would prefer not to touch the fries so he quickly found a way around having to touch them.

We handed the bag of fries back to him and asked him to hand the fries to us at the front, one by one. This was a huge step for him and he complied with our request. Well done Lachlan! This is very good news to tell Debbie.

After the fast-food restaurant we went to the markets and Lachlan had a turn on the giant slide. He jumped up and down at the top of the slide as he was so excited, and when we needed him to stop we signed the "STOP" hand sign. He did stop, thankfully, and sat down. He had around fifteen turns on the slide and then a five-minute turn on the jumping castle. Not in the mood for castles today.

Back home for lunch where Lachlan watched his DVDs from the library. Lachlan ate bread rolls for lunch which he eats every day. He does not get sick of eating the same things over and over for some time, often a number of years. He likes to do that. Lachlan eats the same foods over and over until he eventually becomes sick of them after months or years and then he changes to another food and does the same with that.

After lunch we went to the park for a bike ride with the new tricycle that Lachlan got for Christmas. Wow! He rode it so fast and steered it very well, too. Lachlan's gross motor skills make it harder than usual for him to ride two-wheeler bikes. When he was little he had a tricycle which he loved, but eventually he out grew it.

This new adult size tricycle is perfect for him. It gives him the same independence as other children at the park. He always watches other children riding their bikes at the park, and now he can do the same. The new bike is a big heavy bike, but as Lachlan is big for his age and very strong, he rides it easily.

All of us had so much fun at the park, jogging and riding the bike. It was so great to see Lachlan riding by himself for the first time and he seemed so proud of himself.

At dinner time Lachlan always has pureed food which is an oat mixture containing pureed meat, vegetables and fruit. It does not sound good I know, but Lachlan likes it because all he can taste is banana and oats. I manage to sneak about a cup of vegetables into it as well as meat, fish or eggs. Vitamin supplements are also added.

Lachlan is not willing to eat meat, vegetables or fruit any other way, at this stage. He has eaten some fruit in the past, so maybe he will eat it again at some point in the future. We are very happy that he eats the oat mixture which seems to keep him going and he appears to be healthy enough.

When Lachlan was a baby and would not try new foods, I would sneak other foods such as meat, fruits and vegetables into his custard and he would then eat them. The oat mixture evolved from the custard mix. Sometimes mothers have to be sneaky.

Lachlan played in his room and we read stories as usual with the evening routine. I was hopeful that the exercise of bike riding during the day meant he would sleep well tonight, which he did.

Sunday 11/01/15

Lachlan played on the computer this morning (which he is an expert at using). On the internet, he found a picture of a cartoon he liked the look of in amongst a lot of little pictures and he pointed to the very small wording on the picture and then to the toolbar and I knew this meant that he wanted me to type the words in so he could see what came up about that cartoon. We are always amazed at the ways he finds to communicate.

Sometimes Lachlan studies the spine of DVDs and then points to the name of the manufacturer requesting me to type it into the toolbar so he can investigate. I wish I knew what he was thinking about this. Sometimes he types it himself, but often asks others if they are close by.

It is raining today so off to the indoor markets which Lachlan will enjoy. Lachlan must go out twice a day. He loves going out and does become agitated if he has to stay home all day. He needs a high level of physical activity and has an enormous amount of physical strength and energy. We have a mini trampoline in the lounge room as well as a huge one in the back yard so he can jump whenever he wants. He rarely becomes tired of moving. This keeps the rest of us fit, too, Itsal included.

As for physical strength, Lachlan likes to give some people a big bear hug and sometimes other children can be a bit scared as he does squeeze quite hard at times. We are trying to teach him to be gentle. Lachlan is affectionate and likes hugs from others. We are very grateful that he does not find this kind of touch painful. Quite the opposite in fact.

Getting back to the markets, Lachlan could not resist touching a man's hair. The man had really short spiky hair and without any warning Lachlan reached up and stroked his head. Luckily the man did not turn around or seem to really notice. The market was very crowded and the man just kept on walking with the crowd.

Lachlan also spotted a teenager with a jacket on which must have appealed to him so when we were walking along Lachlan grabbed onto his arm as if to walk with him instead of us. The boy said, "Hi mate," as we were trying to detach Lachlan from his arm. The young man did not seem too concerned about it, and just kept on walking. These kinds of things happen a lot where Lachlan freely expresses what he wants to do and I am always surprised at what people will let him get away with.

This afternoon was too wet to go outside so we decided to go to the toy shop. Just recently Lachlan has begun to re-enter large shopping centres as previously he had found them too overwhelming. Too many people, too many lights, too noisy and busy. Since we have had Itsal (Lachlan's Autism Assistance dog) Lachlan has been much calmer overall. These days Lachlan will hold onto Itsal's harness while walking around in shopping centres, when previously he would just run off if he became overstimulated and overwhelmed.

Having Itsal has made a huge difference and we are so grateful to have him. It has been eight months now since we got Itsal who is the most sedate and patient dog I have ever seen. Lachlan plays rough with him and will often try to ride him like a horse. Itsal simply sits down so that Lachlan is unable to do it. Smart dog! The two of them seem to be able to negotiate between themselves.

There are times when Itsal will just go to another room if he needs a bit of time out, but he is usually not perturbed by things Lachlan does. What a blessing he is!

At the shops today Lachlan rode a children's ride for the first time! He is eight years old. He has always been interested in rides but they have frightened him a little, the movement, noise and lights and sometimes the music they play. Until today he has only ever watched other children on these rides. Lachlan always seemed to like that other children were having so much fun. I cannot count the times other parents have kindly asked me if Lachlan wanted to join the ride with their children.

The parents must have wondered why Lachlan was not joining in on the ride especially when he seemed so excited watching the other children on it. If he saw a ride he was interested in he would always gesture for me to put money in it and he would enjoy watching it go around. I am sure all this must have looked rather strange to onlookers. We are used to that and probably would not even have noticed if people were staring at us.

When out with Lachlan we are always on an interesting mission, a bit like a race horse with blinkers on, I always think. It is fun taking him out especially somewhere he really likes. When he is happy everyone knows as he will jump up and down, shout out and laugh. Sometimes he gives someone a big hug. He does not feel embarrassed about things. He is lucky that way.

Monday 12/01/15

The day started with a trip to the video shop which is one of Lachlan's favourite places to go. He chose two videos and had to wait in a queue which is always a little hard for him to do. He does not like waiting and I do not think he understands why it is necessary for him to do so.

Lachlan does not seem to understand the social rule of waiting his turn in the queue, but he is getting better at waiting. We have noticed this change since he has had Itsal, as Lachlan is much calmer overall. On one of the first shopping outings with Lachlan and Itsal I remember that for the first time Lachlan waited in the pharmacy while a script was being filled. He sat on a chair and Itsal lay on the ground in front at his feet.

It was hard to believe and I had never even tried to get a script filled while Lachlan and I were on an outing before, knowing he would run off if forced to wait. This was excellent!!! As well as waiting for the script, I was able to look around the chemist and found a few other items I wanted to buy. We went to the checkout and there was a long queue. Lachlan jumped up and down, vocalising (as he was in a happy excited mood), but stood in the queue and waited. I was very proud of him as I know this did not make much sense to him. He complied because he knew this was what I wanted, and Itsal seemed to have a calming effect on him which helped greatly.

That same day, we were able to have lunch in the food court, the first time ever for Lachlan and I, while Itsal lay at Lachlan's feet. It was a luxury to sit and have lunch and a break, while Lachlan ate the tops off four or five bread rolls (he only likes the crunchy part) that we had bought from the bakery. Lachlan will not eat anything else from the shopping centre for lunch except bread rolls and they must be crunchy, (funny little guy). Perhaps I may have done this myself when I was a child had I thought I would have been able to get away with it!

Now that Itsal is with us we attract even more attention than before, because everyone likes the look of him. Especially children and older people, even younger people. No, everyone likes him and I can't blame them.

After the video shop, we drove to the park but when we got there Lachlan pointed forward and said, "GO." We knew this meant he did not want to go to the park so we changed plans and headed home. On the way home Lachlan signed the hand sign for "Toilet". Not knowing how urgent his need was, we stopped at a restaurant just in case, but he pointed again and said, "GO," we asked, "Do you want to wait until you get home?" and he pointed ahead and nodded slightly. Sometimes he nods slightly to say yes, but he never says "No" because he does not like the word "No". This was the first time Lachlan had chosen to wait until he got home. He knew what he wanted. His family have always known that. He continually finds ways to communicate his wishes, somehow.

Tuesday 13/01/15

Today Lachlan woke at around 4.30 a.m. Whenever Lachlan wakes up Itsal will come into our bedroom to alert us. Even if Lachlan's pillow falls onto the floor, he comes and wakes us up to let us know something has changed in the room. No longer do we have the worry that Lachlan might wake during the night and try to leave the house. There is no way Itsal would let him do that which is a huge weight of our minds.

Later on in the morning we went to the bakery to buy bread rolls. Each day we buy ten or twelve and Hong (the woman who owns the bakery), makes and keeps them especially for Lachlan each day as she knows they are one of the few foods he will eat. Hong always pays special attention to Lachlan and at times I have heard Lachlan answer her with a reply when she asks, "How are you?" Lachlan sometimes answers, "Good." Lachlan does not answer very many people. He likes Hong who always asks him to put the change in his pocket. He likes this, as he likes helping. Sometimes Lachlan gets a little upset if Hong is not at the bakery when he goes there. Lachlan likes things to be the same every day as then he knows what to expect.

Today Lachlan went to the park to play with his new remote-control car which was a Christmas present. He liked playing with it, but needs a little more practice using the controls. Next, he went to visit Aunty Merri in hospital. We stayed for twenty-five minutes and no longer as Lachlan would have found it hard to stay still and quiet in there. He finds it hard to sit still for too long. Lachlan likes Aunty Merri and is always pleased to see her. He tried to lie in the bed with her which he always does when he visits people in hospital. At times when I have been a patient in hospital Lachlan would always climb into the bed and often go to sleep. He did not mind at all that people were coming in and out of the room.

Sometimes he would want to give one of the nurses a hug there. Every now and then he finds a man, woman or child that he likes enough to want to give them a big hug. He never seems gets a bad response from people. He seems to know who to pick and he always has. We never know when he is going to hug someone, he just does it all of a sudden!

Friday 16/01/15

Today Lachlan visited a playground. It was the second time he had visited this particular playground which has hills covered in rubber, which meant he was able to jump from one hill to another safely. He absolutely loved doing this. Lachlan walked around the playground, himself in one location while Itsal waited in another. This worked out well as Itsal was away from other children in the playground, in his own corner. Children in the park had begun to crowd around Itsal while Lachlan was running around in the park. There were seven children crowding around Itsal, talking to him and all very interested. They did not touch him they just looked and admired him.

Lachlan had noticed a large man sitting on a seat in the park. His three children who were older than Lachlan played in the park, in the distance. Lachlan decided to run over and give the man a big hug. The man said "Hello, little mate," and Lachlan seemed very happy when the man replied. We tried to tear Lachlan away, which made him hang on even tighter to the man's arm. Lachlan found this hilarious and laughed loudly. Eventually we were able to tear him away. This man did not have any visible tattoos, (because Lachlan loves tattoos), but there was something Lachlan really liked about him. I think Lachlan must have very strong gut feelings about people, as he never makes a mistake about who to approach. I wish I knew how he did it.

Sometimes Lachlan will hug other children, but not as often as adults. He does not usually hug children who are unfamiliar to him, but has on a few rare occasions. Lachlan likes to hug his two cousins Billy and Steven, sometimes squeezing Steven who is six months older than Lachlan, a little too hard. Steven always forgives Lachlan and they go back to playing their usual computer and other games. Billy, being five years older, does not seem to mind Lachlan's bear hugs which are incredibly strong. Lachlan loves getting a big squeeze in return and will sometimes request one on his iPad or through his PECS (Picture exchange communication system) folder.

I think that when Lachlan gives people a big squeeze or hug this means that he really wants one. Lachlan finds this sort of pressure on his body calming and he also loves being squeezed in between pillows or blankets.

As Lachlan likes the feeling of being squeezed and held tight, he wears a long cotton sleeping bag to bed, yes even when it is hot and he will not go to sleep without it. He just loves it. My friend at work Shu kindly arranged for a friend of hers to make this latest sleeping bag as Lachlan had grown too big for a shop bought one. I suspect Lachlan likes the feeling of pressure he gets from the sleeping bag. Incredible, but he can actually run in it when he wants to and has never fallen over! He will have to try sack races one day.

Lachlan in his sleeping bag, playing with Itsal.

Monday 19/01/15

Today Lachlan went for a bush walk in the National Park. He saw a fox, rabbits and a hawk as well as some finches. Lachlan liked seeing the huge rabbit and especially the fox. Chickens and pigs are his favourite animals. Next, he went to the park and for the first time Lachlan found other children to play with and took turns with them playing on the giant hamster wheel ride. This was the first time we had seen him play with other children in the park, as Lachlan usually does not take much notice of other children and prefers to play by himself.

While at pre-school Mrs Linda said that he played with other children there, which was wonderful to know. Lachlan seemed to act differently at pre-school, perhaps on his best behaviour. When Lachlan was very young he used to be quite scared of other children at times. It is great to know that things can and do change and we expect even more positive changes in the future.

Once when Lachlan was around six years old he and I were at the park and a little girl approached. The girl sat on the swing next to Lachlan and said "Hi" to him. Lachlan did not usually respond, but this time he said "Hi" back. This was the first time he had ever said "Hi" to anyone. It was as though when the expectation was there, he spoke just like the girl expected. I could not believe it and wondered whether he would keep on saying it now that I knew he could. On another occasion

Lachlan said "Hi" to another friend in the same way. These are the only times he has ever said "Hi". Lachlan is eight and a half years old now.

Lachlan's bedtime routine takes around ninety minutes. First, we play in his room with toys while Lachlan has a snack in his room. Next, we read a story, and put on his sleeping bag, and say prayers. Each night I hold Lachlan's hand until he falls asleep, and tonight was the fastest he had ever fallen asleep- less than five minutes. Tonight, being very tired, Lachlan did not want his usual bedtime story. Itsal lay on his mat on the floor as I held Lachlan's hand and as soon as I left the room, Itsal climbed onto Lachlan's bed where he stayed for the night. They both do if we are lucky.

Saturday 24/01/15

Today Lachlan went to the aquatic centre for a swim with Dad while I waited for Debbie (Itsal's groomer), who came to give Itsal a bath. Lachlan came back home just as Itsal was finishing his bath and set up his DVD player as he had also been to the library to borrow a DVD on the way home. Lachlan had never met Debbie before and he seemed stressed as he saw her and started to make loud vocalisations. I was unsure if he was upset about the DVDs as sometimes Lachlan finds it stressful when a DVD does not work properly or if he was upset because Debbie was at the door.

Debbie asked, "Doesn't he like strangers?" I told her that I thought he was upset about the DVDs. It was nice of her to be concerned about why he was upset. We do not always know the answer, and sometimes we find out later, like this time.

Next Lachlan went to the door and pushed Debbie (not very hard, thankfully) as though to push her out the door, thanks very much and goodbye. Debbie was very understanding and said, "It's OK, mate," and I told Lachlan that everything was fine and that Debbie had come and given Itsal a bath. Lachlan was still a bit stressed about it all, but when I asked him to say, "Thank you" to Debbie he signed "Thank you".

Even though Lachlan seemed disturbed by Debbie's presence, on some level he knew that she was there to help and this was a good thing. I can be sure of this because if he really did not want her there, he would have let all of us know in no uncertain terms! Like he has before with many an electricity sales person. He would have closed the door in her face! Thank goodness he did not do that. There must be a way to keep the door open as the door stopper does not work as Lachlan just takes it out and closes the door. I do hope that Debbie comes back in a month for the next appointment and that she was not offended, but I think she understood. Sorry Debbie.

From Lachlan's perspective, I think that sometimes he sees people as a disturbance or an interruption to whatever he is doing at the time. I am sure he thinks people talk too much and maybe sometimes he is right about that. After all, if he can get by without saying a word, maybe he thinks everyone else should do the same. Sometimes he will say "Shhh" and put his finger over our mouths when he thinks we are talking too much. There have been moments when we have all wished we could do that with someone, so I understand.

Sometimes Lachlan leads us by the hand to the lounge room door and pushes us out the door which his way of letting people know that he would like to be by himself. Occasionally he is busy on the computer doing something that he does not want others to see. That happens sometimes.

Once Lachlan kicked me out of the room and when I quietly crept back to see what he was doing I noticed he was watching a YouTube video which had swear words in the voice over. He knew he would not have been allowed to continue watching it, but for some reason he loved it.

After I signed "Finish" requesting him to find something else to watch, he did. Lachlan often tries to make us happy and he really is fairly compliant with our requests, but not all the time. Hard to imagine any eight-year-old doing every single thing their parents ask without any complaint. That would be a miracle!

Tuesday 27/01/15

Yesterday the countdown started in order to prepare Lachlan for going back to school as today was the second last day of the school holidays. This time I did it a different way. During the holidays Lachlan's school had sent a brief social story in booklet form which told Lachlan who his new teacher would be for the year. The teacher's photo was included in the booklet and it also showed the location of his new classroom in another photo.

As well as the social story the school provided, I made our own on Lachlan's iPad which started three days before he needed to return to school. I wrote at the top of the social story, 'In 3 days Lachlan will be going back to school', and we read the story together. Lachlan likes to have some notice to prepare himself.

Today I changed the social story and we read it once again, - "In 2 days Lachlan will be going back to school". It was obvious by the vocalisations Lachlan made that he was very pleased and excited about going back to school.

Last year Lachlan made a friend who he held hands with (we will call her Chloe). This is very rare and I think it was the first time he had made a real friend at school. Lachlan's teacher sent a photo of the two of them holding hands in class. Everyone thought it was very sweet and when I met Chloe's parents they were equally as pleased that she had made a real friend. Chloe's parents also said that she hardly ever made friends with other children.

Last year Lachlan was invited to a birthday party for the first time which was where we met Chloe's parents. Until this, Lachlan had only ever been to family parties. The invitation came from a girl in Lachlan's class, who we will call Lucy. Lucy had a circus party, complete with a trapeze, clown and jumping castle and Lachlan as well as all of the children, had a wonderful time there. It was really quite exciting that he went to a party as I had heard about some children with autism reaching their teens who had never been invited to a birthday party. I was very pleased that this did not happen to Lachlan.

Lachlan seems to be making friends more at his new school. This is the second year he has been attending his current school. Maybe it is just that he is getting older, but I suspect his current school encourages friendships more as at his previous school he was not allowed to touch the other children.

As it does not come naturally for Lachlan to reach out to people, I am glad that he is allowed physical contact with the other children at the current school, as I think this is very beneficial for his social skills.

Thursday 29/01/15

Lachlan was woken early by his DVD player with the volume turned up very loudly as today was his first day back at school for the year. He woke immediately on hearing the loud music coming from the DVD player, but he seemed happy enough. He watched his DVD for about fifteen minutes until it was time for him to get out of bed. After I called Itsal he happily jumped onto Lachlan's bed and knew exactly what he needed to do. Lachlan sat up and Itsal sat on his pillow which prevented Lachlan from lying back down. Itsal looked very proud as he knew he had done his job.

Strangely enough, Itsal seemed to understand today was the first day back at school as this is the only time we need to hurry Lachlan along so that he is ready for school on time. On weekends Lachlan sleeps in and loves to watch his DVDs in bed for an hour or so after he wakes up.

Lachlan watched a DVD until it was time to go outside and get into the school bus. When he wanted to change the DVD, he signed for 'more' which meant he wanted a suggestion from me for a DVD to watch next. I made four different suggestions and each time he signed 'Finish' to let me know he did not want the ones I had suggested. The fifth one was a winner! Lachlan nodded and took the DVD and watched it for a few minutes until it was time to go to school.

Lachlan has a long trip to school, around forty-five minutes to one hour travelling time. Right on time a black car pulled into our driveway and the usual driver got out and waved to us. He usually drives a van to transport the children to school so as it was a car, this time he asked Lachlan to sit in the middle of the back seat. I assumed there was only one other child to be transported along with Lachlan, and this was the reason for the changed vehicle, but when I asked he said there were two more children to be picked up.

Last year there were also three students, but a van was used to transport the children instead of a car. I worried that Lachlan would not like children sitting so close to him and if he became upset due to a traffic jam or another reason then he may become stressed and anxious and hit out. Maybe the other children would feel the same way and would not like Lachlan sitting next to them either. Today Lachlan was not upset about the vehicle change. In fact, he seemed very happy to go back to his school routine!

As it is a long drive to school, Lachlan has breakfast when he arrives at school as there is no way he would eat and drink earlier in the morning. He likes to take his time finishing a large bottle of water and juice before he starts eating which can take a few hours, so it works best for him to have drinks and food once he arrives at school. Last year the teachers told me that they offered him food and drink first thing in the morning but often he did not want to have anything until morning tea time. He knows what he wants.

In the afternoon, I received an email from Lachlan's teachers telling me that he had a good and happy day for the first day back. I wondered whether the change of teacher would make him feel unsettled, and I know once upon a time it would have. It is great to know that now he can be more flexible when the routine changes. He has eleven children in his class this year.

After school, we went to the shops, park and library. Lachlan was very tired after his first day back and fell asleep easily at 9.30 p.m. after his usual evening routine. This is early for Lachlan.

This is the second year Lachlan has been using assisted school transport. I think he really likes the independence that he feels from using it. He has always enjoyed it and at first we were unsure how it would work out, but thankfully it has worked really well.

Friday 30/01/15

Lachlan was again very excited to go to school and happily carried out every part of his morning routine. He went off to school gladly and easily.

Lachlan's teachers reported that today when asked what he did during the school holidays, Lachlan chose a picture of a swimming pool to explain all the swimming he had enjoyed during the holidays.

The teachers also reported that Lachlan had not eaten much during the day. Tonight, he was still not eating much and seemed extra tired and fell asleep even faster than the night before. His eyes were closed as we said our prayers and he fell asleep. At prayer time Lachlan likes me to say thank you to God for DVDs and always nods his head in agreement when I say this. Sometimes I forget to mention the DVDs in our prayers and he will nod and vocalise, reminding me that I must say thanks for them. After all, DVDs are Lachlan's favourite thing in the whole world, now equal first with Itsal.

Saturday 31/01/15

Lachlan went to visit a local farm today. He was so excited to see coloured chickens which had been dyed pink and blue. Chickens, pigs and horses are his favourite animals (next to Itsal, who is of course impossible to beat). Lachlan loved patting a brown horse, through a gap in the fence.

This reminded me of the time we took Lachlan on a farm stay holiday to country NSW. The four of us went Mum, Dad and Samantha (Lachlan's sister) and all had a great time, especially Lachlan who loved being involved in the daily schedule at the farm. He really enjoyed everything about the farm, he fed the lambs, chickens, horses and dogs and collected eggs each day.

There were two dogs there; one was a working dog a Kelpie who was tied up most of the time except when he was working. The other dog was a Chihuahua who often came to the door of our cabin, looking for attention from us. Lachlan was a bit disturbed about the little visitor. I think he was unsure of what the dog might do. He does not like to be surprised by the things dogs often do such as jump or bark. Lachlan was quite scared of dogs back then, before Itsal came to stay.

The best part of all was when Lachlan had a pony ride. He was so excited, verbalising making happy noises. When we returned home he would watch the iPad video of himself riding the pony over and over and would be just as excited each and every time he watched it.

A few months before when we were planning the farm stay holiday, we had some discussions about it. Around that time I took Lachlan to a local shopping centre and we found a miniature farm inside with some farm animals for children to pat. Lachlan wanted to enter the enclosure through the small fence and interact with the animals inside it. After a while he laid down in the hay which covered the floor. I wondered what he was doing as I had never seen him do that before. When I asked him to stand up he pulled my hand, pulling my body down toward to floor of the mini farm. Next, he made a sound, (imitating a snoring sound) and I realised that he thought this was the farm stay he had heard us talking about. How funny! I also then knew how thrilled he would be to stay at a real farm!

Chapter 2
February 2015

Tuesday 03/02/15

Lachlan had a great day at school today and I think he really likes his new class. Since the new school year started he has been really happy getting into the school bus in the mornings. He is always the first student to be picked up and two other children are also picked up along the way. Lachlan knew one of the boys from last year, along with the driver, which is good as he prefers things to stay the same. These days Lachlan is able to cope with some changes to his routine, a lot more than when he first started school three years ago.

Tonight and last night, Lachlan came into the kitchen and watched as I blended his dinner. He covered his ears trying to block the noise from the blender. While I was blending his food, he touched the label of the milk carton which he also did last night. He is usually not interested in watching me make food and rarely comes in to see what is being made. I wondered whether Lachlan liked touching the milk carton because it was cold. "That's milk, do you want to try some?" I asked. Lachlan touched the label again. I also touched the label myself, trying to figure out the reason he was so interested in it. Then I realised what he was doing. The milk carton said 'A2 milk, feel the difference', and that is exactly what he was doing, feeling the label to see if it was different. Literal thinking!

This reminded me of a time when I had taken washing off the line and was carrying the full basket inside. Lachlan had been playing outside in the backyard and I asked him to help by opening the door as my hands were full with the heavy basket. Lachlan had not held a door open for me before this but I thought it was worth a try. He opened the door and walked inside to the lounge room to play, leaving the door to slam behind him (and on me with my basket!). Funny! He did do what he was asked which was to open the door, but didn't think of the next step quite the way I thought he would. Lucky I wasn't being chased by a lion or a savage dog! But I was grateful that he listened and carried out my request.

Friday 06/02/15

Lachlan has just finished his first full week at school for the year. It could not have gone any better. He just loves his new class and loves going to school now. What a huge relief it is when he is happy! When Lachlan is happy, everyone is happy! When I unpacked Lachlan's school bag I noticed that he had received an award certificate for a wonderful start in his new class.

I remember the day that Lachlan started at school back in kindergarten. He was so distressed about having to stay inside such a small classroom, with really not much to do. One of the teachers said that some of the children needed to get used to being inside a classroom, but Lachlan was well past that having been to preschool for two years previously as well as early intervention preschool in the year before starting school. There was no structure in the class room that day and Lachlan really needed it to be more structured. The other children were running around in the classroom and it was very noisy. There were a few toys on the ground, some trains which another boy was playing with and he clearly did not want Lachlan anywhere near them which was obvious as he snatched them into his fists when Lachlan went to look at them.

Before Lachlan started preschool, he went to two playgroups. One was a special needs group, staffed by speech therapists, occupational therapists, teachers, physiotherapists and social workers. Here the children were introduced to PECS (Picture Exchange Communication System) giving them the idea that requests could be represented in PECS pictures. Whenever they played with a toy they would be shown a matching PECS picture. This way they would learn to make choices using the PECS pictures. Lachlan seemed to pick up how to use them very quickly and he really enjoyed using them. We started a PECS folder at home with photos of Lachlan's favourite foods and toys. It didn't take long before he was an expert at using it to request his wants and needs and I was so pleased that he had this new way to communicate.

The other group which Lachlan attended was run by a local church. They had a structured play session and morning tea. Next the children sang some songs and played outside, which taught the children to share bikes and other toys with each other.

Getting back to the first day of school – Wow that was so stressful! I stayed in the classroom with him the entire day, not wanting to leave knowing he would be distressed if I did. The teachers suggested I leave twice and tried to reassure me that all would be well once I left. As a mother, it just did not feel right and I ignored what the teachers said to me and stayed anyway. I did not even go to the bathroom that whole day because I knew that Lachlan would have become distressed if I had left him in the new environment with people he did not know. You need a good bladder when you have a child with autism as there is not always the opportunity to go to the bathroom!

The next day, my husband Chris offered to take Lachlan to school knowing how upsetting I had found the day before. The next day was a little better but Chris said Lachlan had cried when he left him in the classroom. Chris waited in the school office for half an hour until they phoned the classroom to check on Lachlan. They reported that Lachlan had stopped crying and that he had settled.

Little by little Lachlan became used to going to school, never really liking it very much and he would have much preferred to stay home. Sometimes he would hide his school clothes, as he thought this would mean that he would not have to go to school. Each day I drove Lachlan to an out-of-area school which took around forty minutes and I drove to work afterwards. I was able to start work later which meant I had enough time to arrive at school and work on time. At this stage I knew Lachlan would not have tolerated the transport service provided by the school. First, he had to get used to going to school and maybe at some later stage he could try out the transport service.

Lachlan went to that school for two years and he never really liked it any more than when he first started. Each day he would want to stay in the car and not want to get out, holding onto the seat. I wondered if that would ever change, and in two years, it never really did. Each day was the same when it came to getting out of the car and it was heart-breaking.

Lachlan started back at school one week ago and I really cannot believe how far he has come and how much he has changed since he first started school. Even changes to the school transport this year did not bother him at all. The bus route needed to be changed due to a new student being picked up along the way, but this has not bothered Lachlan at all.

When Lachlan was younger he really could not tolerate any changes to his routine. Changes to his usual routines would cause him to have a meltdown. These days he adjusts to changes so much better. It is great to know that things can change and I am looking forward to seeing how he will be in another five years from now and in another ten years.

Saturday 07/02/15

Today we restarted our outdoor spa which we have not used since Lachlan was born. I guess we thought he would want to go in it all the time and rather than have the temptation there, we drained the water from it and it has not been used for around ten years. Sometimes it would fill up with rain water and Lachlan would paddle his feet in it. It is not very deep. Lachlan was so happy when the spa was restarted and spent a few hours in it this afternoon.

Lachlan listened to a CD in his room as part of his bedtime wind down. He likes to listen to the same part in a song and likes to play it over and over. Lachlan likes it when people sing, and he does not mind if people are not good singers. He likes any type of singing – good, bad or otherwise. He will usually sign for "More". Sometimes he will touch people's mouths as though he is wondering how the sound is coming out. He does not seem sad that he cannot sing, he is just happy that other people do. He has a plastic microphone and when he sings he makes a sound "Oo" or "Ee". He is having just as much fun as any other children I have seen singing. A workmate once suggested I take him to karaoke. Good idea I thought, he would love that. Lachlan seemed more tired than usual after all the spa swimming and fell asleep easily.

Sunday 08/02/15

Today we went to church. Lachlan sat next to me for some time during the service and he loved the singing and watching the band playing musical instruments. Everyone knows Lachlan at church and people were genuinely pleased to see him there. Nobody minds if he makes noise or eats his bread rolls during the service. Lachlan helps makes other people feel comfortable at church if their children are noisy.

Back into the spa for the afternoon. Lachlan gestured for Itsal to join him in the spa. When I asked Itsal to enter the spa he put his two front paws on the first step. Itsal was hesitant to go any further, knowing he may have slipped on the wet steps. What a smart fellow he is! He waited and watched over Lachlan while he played in the spa.

This evening I went into Lachlan's room to begin his wind down routine. As usual for his routine, he played in his room. This evening he played with a musical mat on the floor which had piano keys. The idea is that the player stands on the correct keys to construct a song. Lachlan stood on the right keys and played a song. As I watched I was a little surprised that Lachlan knew how to play a song and wondered if Dad had shown him how to do this. When asked, Dad said he had not showed him, so Lachlan figured it out himself somehow. We often do not know how Lachlan learns but once he learns a task he does not forget it as he has such an excellent memory.

Lachlan attended music therapy which was part of an early intervention group when he was two years old and he has loved music ever since. He loves classical music and all types of musical instruments. He likes to listen to classical music especially in the car and he will often point to the CD he wants to play. He knows exactly which songs are on each one, in which order for the whole collection. He remembers things like that.

Friday 13/02/15

Today we slept in as the alarm did not work which left only twenty minutes for Lachlan to prepare before the school bus arrived. Panic! Today he is having his first swimming lesson at school for the year and he has been looking forward to it as his teacher had been talking about it. After a huge rush, he managed to join the school bus on time.

Speaking of rushing I reminded myself of a day last week when I fed Itsal twice because I was in a rush and forgot that I had already fed him. Funny, because he just sat in front of the food, not eating it and looking at me. I always know I have done something wrong when he stops and waits. Itsal sat for ten minutes waiting for me to realise my mistake. After lots of encouragement he was still hesitant but slowly began to eat the food.

Lachlan likes his morning routine to go as planned, the same each day. After I told Lachlan that we were running late and he needed to get straight up out of bed, I was very pleased that today he complied with my request. He usually prefers to take his time, but today he understood that he needed to hurry before the school bus showed up to take him to school. He seemed happier than usual, perhaps because he had more sleep than usual.

When Lachlan was a baby, he did not sleep very well and I remember somebody had told me that 'white noise' helped babies to sleep. I thought it was worth a try as we were all so tired. We would turn on the vacuum cleaner and one night we all fell asleep and woke up three hours later with the vacuum cleaner still running! It seemed to work, so we did that again from time to time.

After Lachlan came home from school, he was very happy to have another swim in the spa which did not seem to tire him at all as he woke during the night and stayed awake for about three hours. Sometimes this happens, but much less than it did when he was younger. As tomorrow is not a school day, it did not matter very much.

When Lachlan wakes during the night he is usually happy and he can be heard vocalising. He usually does not get out of his bed but mostly will require settling back down to sleep by someone sitting on the chair in his room, sometimes holding his hand.

Saturday 14/02/15

Lachlan went out to the shops and his favourite place, the library. After lunch, he had a swim in the spa, which he enjoyed once again. He is able to swim as he has had swimming lessons for the past five years. He is not having them this term as he was very distracted last term, so we thought that having a break for a term may be just what he needs. He had been having the lessons one on one with a fabulous instructor who really knows how to bring out the best in him. Recently another child joined in on the swimming lesson and Lachlan seemed to have lost a bit of focus.

The year before last Lachlan participated in a junior surfing group at the beach and loved being part of it. After the group session, he would swim at the beach. He loved being thrown around in the sea by the big waves. The rougher the better for him and even if he was pulled under he just got back up and continued on. He is not scared at all of the waves. He loves the beach and everything about it. He loves playing in the sand.

Tonight after dinner, Lachlan played on the computer. He pressed lots of keys at once, but looked as though he knew what he was doing. He had split the screen in half and on one side he played videos of trains which he had found on a website. He had selected the ones he wanted to view and watched them one by one. Meanwhile on the other side of the screen, he typed words into Google to search for more videos he liked. Next, I noticed one small video played in the middle of the screen in the background.

He worked this out himself and I have no idea how. He always seems to understand how things are stored in the computer and knows exactly how to back track to a previous place. Everything about the computer stays in Lachlan's amazing memory. He figures out how to locate information starting at a particular point – A to B to C etc. and then is able to remember the paths. I do not know how to do the same.

Tonight, during Lachlan's evening routine, we sang and signed a song about rainbows. Lachlan remembered all the colour signs and signed them as we sang. Rainbows are another one of his favourite things and once when he was much younger we saw the most beautiful rainbow right outside of our front window. Lachlan was so excited and stared at it for a very long time. The next day Lachlan looked out the window to find the rainbow again. He looked at me and signed the 'more' sign, wanting me to bring the rainbow back. I did not think this had anything to do with his autism and that it was one of those cute things which children say, believing their parents can do anything at all. It was a bit like the times he has wanted us to kiss his hand which was hurt. Lachlan will also ask his teachers to do this if he injures himself at school. He is not embarrassed; he just wants someone to kiss his sore better so that he can get back to playing.

Thursday 19/02/15

Today the morning routine went very well, but just as the school bus arrived, Lachlan jumped onto the lounge chair and lay face down. He placed his head in the corner of the lounge so that I was unable to see his face. I asked him to stand up and told him that the bus had come to take him to school. He reluctantly walked out the door clinging to my arm on the way to the van. When he sat in his usual seat, he lay down for a few seconds then got up again. The driver asked me if he was feeling alright and I told him that I thought that perhaps he was tired.

After Lachlan went on his way I wondered about his reluctance to go into the school bus. Could he be sick? He seemed otherwise fine so I was unsure. When Lachlan is coming down with something he usually stops eating and drinking enough for us to notice. Sometimes he will be lethargic and lay around instead of playing and being his usual active and happy self.

Now that the day is over and I did not hear from the school, I guessed that Lachlan must have been more tired than unwell. The other day we heard that Lachlan fell asleep at school so perhaps he is getting used to the early morning starts again.

After dinner Lachlan usually jumps on the trampoline. The amount of time which he is able to jump for is unbelievable. Well over one hour! He has an incredible amount of energy and he is extremely strong as well. One day when Lachlan was half way through eating his dinner, he requested to go outside. Not knowing what he wanted we followed him outside and onto the trampoline. From this night on Lachlan would eat half his dinner and then ask to go on the trampoline! We have to be very careful what we start off and agree to as Lachlan likes the established routine to stay the same and would become upset if we tried to change it.

We did change it however as Lachlan has just started eating all of his dinner again before asking for the trampoline. He likes company on the trampoline and will ask anyone who is around at the time to join him. Lachlan does not think anyone is too old, too sick or too unfit to jump with him. He has heard just about very reason or excuse from people but he will still lead people by the hand hoping they will be willing to jump with him. He really loves it when someone agrees. Lachlan can out jump anyone as it takes a very long time before he gets tired.

Lachlan is a fast runner too. I remember once when Lachlan and I were at the park. It was a small park which was enclosed by a fence and backed onto an oval. Lachlan played on the swing and had fun running all around the park. All of a sudden Lachlan squeezed through a tiny gap in the fence and ran up a hill onto the oval. He was running as fast as he could until I could no longer see him as he had gone up and over the hill. Being too big to squeeze through the gap in the fence, luckily I saw a couple on the oval who must have been watching the football game. They seemed to have some idea of what had happened and they watched as Lachlan ran as fast as he could onto the football oval. They knew I was unable to see Lachlan from where I stood at the bottom of the hill. Knowing that I could not stop Lachlan, I asked the man to grab him. He asked me "What's his name?" and I gave it, but also suggested that the best thing to do was to just pick him up. The man looked a little confused, but did as I asked. Lachlan was laughing when the man picked him up. He just thought it was funny! I was so grateful that this couple had been there watching the football game just at the right time and that this man had been so helpful. He commented, "He would make a great footy player one day. He is such a fast runner!"

In order for me to have accessed the oval I would have had to go to the exit on the other side of the park, and by then who knows where Lachlan would have been, so I was very pleased things worked out the way they did. Thank you very much to that couple whoever you are.

Friday 20/02/15

Today Itsal woke me by placing his paw near me on the bed. It was 5.30am and I could hear Lachlan awake in his room. I assumed this was the reason Itsal had woken me, to let me know. What a relief it is to know that Lachlan is being protected by Itsal and would not be able to wander off while his family are asleep unaware.

There is a plus side when Lachlan wakes early as he is happy to begin the school routine, having had some time in his room to get used to the idea. I asked him if he would like his DVD player and he nodded. Sometimes when he is tired he will take the DVD out of the player and put it under his pillow and go back to sleep. Luckily today he was happy to watch the DVD and then get out of bed to prepare for school. Today was swimming day at school and Lachlan was very pleased when I reminded him of this as he loves swimming. He seemed really excited to go to school.

Lachlan returned home in a happy mood and after afternoon tea (which is always a chocolate chip muffin from a particular shop which I had bought in advance and frozen), he went to the library and shopping. Today Lachlan signed, "Thank you" and "Goodbye" to the librarian without having to be asked. We were very proud of him.

During the evening routine, we read a story about farm animals and afterwards I begun to sign each animal saying, "I am a ...whatever the animal was" and then doing the sign for it. After I had signed "Duck", "Cow" and "Horse" Lachlan reminded me the next time when I said, "I am a ...". Lachlan did the sign for "Girl". Lately he has been signing "Girl" and "Boy" a lot. Perhaps they had been talking about girls and boys at school, so Lachlan wanted to remind me of which one I am.

Saturday 21/02/15

This morning was a bush walk in the National Park and this afternoon on the way to another park Lachlan started to give directions by pointing and saying "Go". Knowing that he had something in mind, we followed his requests as we were interested to find out what it was. We did not know where he would take us. He took us out of our local area. After a series of turns we realised that Lachlan had taken us to a new supermarket which had just opened. We did not know it was there. We wondered how he knew about it but we do know that when Lachlan sees something he does not forget it. I wondered if he had seen it in the past as we had driven down that street, perhaps while it was being built. But how would he know that a building would become a supermarket? Maybe there had been a sign there and he remembered. Who knows?

Lachlan had a firm idea of what he wanted to do inside the supermarket. He led us to the bakery section and after inspecting the bread rolls he chose a really long baguette bread roll which was almost as tall as him. He started to wave it around like a baton and I was pleased that he did not knock anyone out with it. It was quite funny, I thought. Once outside he started eating it and it reminded me of someone playing a didgeridoo as it was so big. Lachlan knew exactly what he wanted.

Sunday 22/02/15

This morning when making a smoothie Lachlan came into the kitchen to investigate. He does not like the noise that the blender makes, but he was interested to see what I was mixing as this is also how I mix his dinner each night. The smoothie was a purple colour as it had blueberries in it. I asked Lachlan if he would help by tipping it from the mixing jug into a glass and he nodded in agreement. After I handed him the jug he tipped the smoothie into the glass. I did not offer to assist him as I thought it best for him to practice pouring.

Lachlan poured the smoothie into the glass, overfilling it and causing some of to spill out onto the counter. I said, "Thanks for helping" and did not mention the spill as I could tell Lachlan was slightly unhappy about the spillage.

Lachlan looked very excited when I drank some of the smoothie especially since it was purple, his favourite colour. I wondered if Lachlan would drink these in the future. We have to take it very slow with introducing Lachlan to new food or drinks because if he finds anything about them unpleasant he will never be interested in trying them. He has never liked drinking milk, but you never know he may try it sometime in the future. Lachlan's speech therapist who we are working with on the food issues says the best way to present foods is to leave them around where he can easily see them or see other people eating them. This is the way he will become used to seeing the foods around and hopefully he will become less resistant to them.

This afternoon Lachlan went shopping and liked the look of a children's train ride. He showed his excitement by jumping up and down. Lachlan has always liked seeing other children on rides but he has never been interested in riding them himself. Only once before has he ever wanted to ride on a children's ride in a shopping centre. He has always been wary of rides but likes them at the same time.

Lachlan has been invited many times by other children and their mothers to join in on rides. When this happens, I explain that he just likes to watch. Often we will see children come and go on rides and Lachlan likes watching them having fun. Sometimes I think Lachlan would like to join in on the rides, but I suspect he finds them too stimulating with the lights, noise and movement all happening at the same time.

Today this changed when Lachlan examined a children's train ride from many different angles and then decided to have a ride on it! This was just the second time he has ever done this so we were very pleased that he could enjoy something that most other children do without being overwhelmed by it. We want him to have fun on the ride and today he did.

Monday 23/02/15

Lachlan woke at 4.19 a.m. Sometimes this happens and we do not really know why. Lachlan is always in a happy mood when he wakes. I could hear him laughing as he played with Itsal in his room. When I checked on Lachlan there did not appear to be any reason for his waking. From experience, I knew It was unlikely that he would go back to sleep. Lachlan continued to play with Itsal until around 6.00 a.m. when I took Lachlan's DVD player into his room which he watched until it was time to get dressed for school.

Next door there is a construction site and we could hear that the workers had started work early. Lachlan heard the workmen talking so selected a Bob the Builder DVD for himself to watch. While it played he found a yellow plastic work hat which he remembered was in his toy box.

When the van arrived to pick Lachlan up for school he was still wearing the yellow hat which he wore once inside the van as he wanted to wear it to school. He loves dressing up and I remember when he was at preschool

Mrs Linda told me that he liked dressing up in a tutu and he would dance around for the other children. They thought it was funny, and Lachlan probably did too. Sometimes in his preschool years he would want to wear my nightie over his own pyjamas and then he would jump on the bed with it on. Not sure what he was thinking about that, but he was having fun.

Tuesday 24/02/15

All went well with the morning school routine and afterwards Lachlan went to the library to borrow a DVD. He chose one about a cast of comical characters which was the same brand as a collection of small books he had at home which he was quite fond of. Lachlan likes me to read the names of all the characters on the back cover of the book.

Lachlan always describes himself as the happy character when I ask him which character he thinks is most like him. Wanting to know what he thought, I went on and asked him which character he thought was most like his sister Samantha. He pointed to the character with long rubbery arms who liked to tickle people.

Next, I asked which one was like me and Lachlan pointed to the optimistic sunny character (thank goodness!). When asked about Dad he pointed to the accident-prone character who was covered in bandages, unsure why a man covered in bandages represented his Dad, but perhaps because the two of them often jump on the trampoline together? Next, I asked Lachlan which character he thought was most like his Nanna and he pointed to the bewildered character. Mum is not reading books these days which is lucky for Lachlan and myself as we would both be in such a lot of trouble over that! Maybe Nanna would see the funny side of it.

This evening Lachlan was very interested in cheese slices which he has eaten previously as a toddler. As he has eaten them before, there is more of a chance he will start eating them again (according to Debra who is helping with food issues). This would be fantastic as Lachlan's diet is very restricted at the moment as he only eats a few foods.

For some reason Lachlan is more open to trying new foods while he is in the bath perhaps because there is no expectation for him to eat them while in there. After all, people usually do not eat while they are taking a bath. While in the bath, Lachlan takes a piece of cheese and touches it, licks it and breaks it up and puts it in the bath. Debra says it is good if Lachlan does this as touching the food is a step toward him trying that food. Sometimes he will want a nearby person to eat the food and places it in their mouth as though he is filling a garbage bin. He thinks this is funny! If I tell Lachlan I do not want it, he will place it in the bin if requested but he thinks human mouth bins are much more fun!

Thursday 26/02/15

All is well with the school routine and this afternoon Lachlan went shopping at our local centre which he likes as it is very familiar to him. He knows where everything is there. Yes, EVERYTHING in each shop because he can remember each item. It is all stored in his little computer like memory.

We walked past a café where a man was sitting drinking coffee. Lachlan must have liked the look of his white hair which was thick and very curly around the sides with a bald spot in the middle. Before there was time to do anything about it, Lachlan walked past the man and reached out and ruffled his white hair. I instructed Lachlan to put his hands down which he did and finally removed them from the man's white hair. The man just smiled, luckily.

Lachlan is fascinated by anyone with interesting or unusual hair and there is never any warning that he may try to touch their hair. I am grateful that so far people have been very understanding about this. Thank you to the man with the curly white hair.

Speaking of hair, I was reminded of one time we were visiting family and Lachlan's teenage cousin Daniel and his friend were sitting and chatting at a table outside near the pool. Lachlan walked around happily looking at different things in the yard such as a football and pool toys. All of a sudden, out of the blue and from behind, Lachlan ruffled and pulled Daniel's friend's hair.

I think he pulled it quite hard and the boy seemed a little surprised about it, but thought it was funny. Lucky he was so easy going about it. This is one of the ways which Lachlan expresses excitement, so if he likes you he might ruffle your hair. You can see how happy and excited he is when he does this and he chooses his targets very carefully. It always amazes me that people are so understanding about this.

When Lachlan visits Daniel he will often open his door, and go and jump on his bed. Thankfully he was not asleep but just chatting to friends in his room unlike the last time Lachlan done this when he was asleep. This time Lachlan joined in on whatever Daniel and his friends were doing in there.

Sometimes Lachlan finds a DVD in Daniel's room. One time he found a horror movie in there and wanted to take it home. Family are always very accommodating and said he could borrow it, not liking to see him upset if they said no, so it came home. We are not worried about him watching horror movies as we know he will watch the section at the very start and that will probably be all. Lachlan put it in the DVD collection with the rest and when we have had visitors some of them have noticed it and asked whether Lachlan was allowed to watch horror movies, which of course, he would not be. It just looks that way being in the pile with the rest of them.

Lachlan does not see scary things in the same way as lots of other children. Once when we were visiting Lachlan's cousin Steven who is six months older than Lachlan, Steven appeared wearing an ugly mask which I think he had bought from the Easter show. I was startled by seeing Steven in the mask, but Lachlan made no reaction to it at all. He was not frightened by it, only interested and wanted to touch it. Lachlan really does not mind what people look like, and if someone really looked like the mask it would make no difference to him. It is all the same to him. Nice to know.

The way that Lachlan used to interact with his cousin Mathew was something really special. Mathew sustained a serious brain injury when he was just sixteen years old, before Lachlan was born. After Mathew's car accident, he was unable to walk, talk or eat and had to be fed through a tube. He needed to use a wheelchair and he was often drowsy or asleep. He was in hospital for years and at first was more responsive and had the use of one of his arms. At this stage Mathew was able nod to communicate and therefore answer a question.

As time went on Mathew lost the use of his arm and he became less responsive and seemed to be drowsier. Mathew lived with this brain injury for eight years before he passed away at age twenty-four. Of course, losing Mathew was totally devastating for the whole immediate and extended family.

When Lachlan was born Mathew came to visit us in hospital and when Lachlan was placed on his lap in his wheelchair, he smiled. We would place Lachlan on Mathew's lap whenever they seen each other and as Lachlan grew he became very used to Mathew. Lachlan would climb onto his wheelchair and want to sit on the footplates. At times Lachlan would sit on Mathew's feet.

Sometimes Lachlan would jump up and down on the footplates and the wheelchair would shake. Lachlan thought this was cool. Mathew would smile and even laugh sometimes. Lachlan was rough with him, but Mathew seemed to enjoy it – no gentle treatment just because he was in a wheelchair!

Lachlan would turn Mathew's head around to face him, wanting Mathew to interact with him. I think that Lachlan was wanting Mathew to talk to him or play with him. Mathew did acknowledge Lachlan by smiling although Lachlan seemed to expect more at times. Mathew was amused by this. You could see it on his face as he always looked so delighted. Lachlan did not have any less expectations of Mathew than he had of anyone else and he did not have any preconceived ideas about Mathew because he looked or seemed different to others. He did not consider all the things that Mathew could not do anymore. Lachlan saw what he could do and made the most of that, and Lachlan adored him.

Friday 27/02/15

Today was a pupil free day so no school for Lachlan. I took a drink into Lachlan's room while he stayed in bed watching his DVD. I could not believe that he said the word "Drink" after I put it down. I am always totally amazed when Lachlan speaks and I always wonder why he sometimes says a word once and does not keep on saying it. Maybe it is just really hard for him to do. I have always had the feeling it is a struggle for Lachlan to talk, but every now and then he does speak. His family are so happy just to hear him say one word.

There was a meeting on at school for parents this afternoon so Samantha (Lachlan's sister) offered to stay and play with Lachlan. Samantha and I chatted on the phone before she arrived and she told me that she had been offered a new job, which she was very excited about.

Lachlan heard me talking to Samantha and he also seemed really excited. I told Lachlan the news and asked him what he thought about that. When I offered him the phone he said "Go" to Samantha. He was also pleased for her. Even though he does not say many words he confirmed that he understood what we were talking about. I could see by his physical reaction that he was very excited. He jumped up and down. Next Samantha spoke to him and he said "Go" again. We assume that Lachlan understands most things even though he is non-verbal. He takes everything in even though there may seem to be no response from him at times.

After Samantha arrived she and Lachlan went to the local shops and Lachlan returned with a DVD which he was very pleased about. Samantha said the afternoon had went well and the two of them had jumped lots on the trampoline.

In the evening Lachlan said a lot of words. I would say a word then he would repeat it – Mum, Dad, Sam, Dog, and Itsal. The words "Sam", "Dog" And "Itsal" were not completely clear but he made a good effort. The words Mum and Dad were clear. Good Trying Lachlan!

Chapter 3
March 2015

Tuesday 03/03/15

Today after Lachlan went to school there was a speech therapy session to discuss the plan with Lachlan's eating. He has made great progress with these sessions and has expanded on the foods he eats to a large degree.

Debra who is Lachlan's speech therapist has helped Lachlan to branch out the range of foods he eats to include other foods very similar to the ones he already eats and likes. From there we keep on branching out. He now eats different types of bread rolls and crackers instead of just the one type of each. He is slowly changing his diet to include more and more foods. It is a relief to know that things can change for the better.

Until Lachlan started the sessions with Debra, I had no idea how to expand the range of foods he ate. Now I understand that it has to be a very gradual shift whereby one small element changes at a time; for instance, a long bread roll with sesame seeds to the same bread roll without sesame seeds.

Debbie said that the reason Lachlan has not become tired of his dinner is because I vary it as much as I can. Debbie also said that using different plates/bowls would help Lachlan to see it differently, so that he does not become tired of eating it. There needs to be a fine balance with his food between it being a little different, and being different enough to keep him interested. If it is too different Lachlan will see it as another food and will not eat it.

Lachlan came home from school in a happy mood. A few days ago, we had asked Lachlan through his iPad if he had seen his friend Chloe from last year. At the time we asked about Chloe, Lachlan said that he had not seen her, but today we heard that Lachlan had found Chloe at school and they played together in the playground. Last year Lachlan and Chloe held hands in class.

When we spoke at home about meeting up with Chloe, Lachlan seemed so thrilled to have found his friend again. When Lachlan was younger we wondered if he would ever make a friend as he seemed uninterested and even a little frightened by other children. Now we know he can and does make friends with other children. What a fantastic change for him!

Wednesday 04/03/15

After school today Lachlan was booked in for a haircut with Danielle. Danielle is Lachlan's hairdresser and when it is time for Lachlan's haircut Danielle and Lachlan move outside onto the verandah as this is where the hair cutting takes place. An occupational therapist had told me previously that outside was the best place for Lachlan to have his hair cut as he then would not associate another room in the house with a stressful experience, which made a lot of sense to me.

Lachlan has come such a long way with hair cutting since Danielle has been doing his hair. At first Linda who first met Lachlan as his support educator at preschool, would come along with Danielle (Danielle is Linda's daughter) for the haircut. Linda and Danielle were a fantastic team and Linda was able to help by calming Lachlan while Danielle did the haircut.

Each haircut day we prepare Lachlan by showing him visuals of Danielle, scissors and a present. Danielle brings Lachlan a present every time she comes to do his hair, and he looks forward to that.

Today Lachlan tolerated the hair cut with hardly any distress. Toward the end he wanted to go and begin his bath which he usually has after his haircut to wash away all the loose hair. Lachlan patted Itsal today while he was having his hair cut and this seemed to calm his mood.

Lachlan has always found it uncomfortable to have his hair cut. Lachlan's head seems to be sensitive and he experiences sensory overload from the loose hair falling on him. He has learned to tolerate haircuts very well through Danielle's perseverance. Thank you, Danielle, you have made a huge difference. Thank you, Linda, for your excellent suggestion that Danielle cut Lachlan's hair at home. More about Linda later.

Before Danielle became Lachlan's hairdresser, he needed to visit a hair salon. I had tried to trim it myself at home and Lachlan had become very distressed by this and I could not bear to persist knowing how much he disliked it. He seemed so frightened. Next, I tried cutting his hair while he was asleep. This happened a few times and as I am not a hairdresser, Lachlan ended up with some very interesting and crooked looking hair styles which show up sometimes in old photos.

When Lachlan was around two years old I decided that I needed to start taking him to the hairdresser as his hair was very thick and I had not found a way I could successfully cut it at home. It was a very stressful experience for all involved. Lachlan would have to stand inside a shopping trolley so that he would not run away. Each time he had a haircut, I would always buy some new toys to try to distract him while his hair was being cut. Nothing really worked, but having some chocolate chip biscuits to eat at least kept his hand busy so they could not be used to push the hairdresser away. Lachlan would scream and cry the whole time and I noticed the hairdresser's hands trembled while she was cutting his hair.

On haircut days, I would always buy the hairdresser a present to give to her afterwards as I know she also found the haircuts very stressful just as Lachlan and I had. When Lachlan first started having haircuts with Danielle it was instantly better than having to take him to the salon, perhaps because he was at home, and also because Danielle had such a calm and relaxed manner. Danielle was always really wonderful with Lachlan and this helped greatly to relax him. These days, haircuts are fine with Danielle. Lachlan has learned to tolerate them and now his hair always looks fantastic!

These are the visuals we use for Lachlan's haircut:

Today at school Lachlan played with his buddy from a nearby school. His buddy was an older boy perhaps eleven or twelve years of age. Lachlan became very excited when we spoke about this. Lachlan likes older children, particularly boys, so the buddy experience suited him perfectly. Two weeks ago we received some photos of Lachlan interacting with his buddy. He looked so happy playing with him. The photos show the two of them saying "Hi" by touching hands and Lachlan leading his buddy by taking hold of his arm. It looked quite funny, as though Lachlan had taken a hostage and it was obvious by the photo that Lachlan really liked his buddy. Another photo showed Lachlan climbing up onto some play equipment with his buddy watching on. It is great relief to know that Lachlan now enjoys the company of other children.

At school recently they have been practicing leaving an apple on Lachlan's table so that he becomes used to seeing it around. Debbie said that the first step towards him eating an apple or other food is by him becoming de-sensitized to seeing it, at first. The next step would be Lachlan touching it. The first step is going well so far. Lachlan has eaten apples in the past so hopefully he will go back to eating them. We shall see. I have learned not to become stressed about Lachlan's food choices as I do all that I am able and the rest is up to him. When I bought these diet issues up to the paediatrician he said that Lachlan would not be the size and weight he was if he were not eating enough. Hearing that comment helped me to relax and not worry so much about Lachlan's diet. Lachlan seems big and healthy despite his restricted food choices so far.

The evening routine is running slightly late but Itsal always seems to know the time. He comes over and gently grabs my wrist with his mouth and he leads me to his food bowl reminding me that his dinner is half an hour late.

Each evening Lachlan feeds Itsal and Itsal will not eat the food until Lachlan says "Go". Once Itsal was home and with me for some reason and Lachlan was out somewhere and came home late. I fed Itsal at the usual time but as I was getting his food together I wondered what would happen now that Lachlan was not home to say "Go". Itsal just sat for a while and I needed to encourage him by asking him to eat his dinner a few times. Itsal knew this was an unusual change to the routine but eventually he ate his food.

Itsal's feeding time is around the same time on weekdays each morning and evening. On weekends it can be later and sometimes Itsal will lead me to his food bowl if he wants to remind me that he thinks his dinner is late. We never really forget about him but at times we get busy doing other things, so I am glad he reminds me.

Friday 06/03/15

This evening the bedtime routine in Lachlan's room included reading some books, doing some reading homework and playing dominos. Lachlan has a domino tower and when a marble is put in the top and makes its way to the bottom of the tower, it is released from the tower pushing down the entire row of dominos. Lachlan is slightly disturbed when the line of dominos stops short and some of them fail to fall down. He likes it to all work perfectly, so to him they should all fall down. Lachlan makes a slight sigh letting me know he was a little disappointed that all the dominos did not fall like they should have. The next time I did it I tried to line them up better so that they all fell, but again the dominos stopped short of falling over halfway through the row. Itsal nudged the rest of the dominos with his so nose so that they fell. I found it incredible that he knew to do this to prevent Lachlan becoming disturbed. Smart dog Itsal!

Saturday 07/03/15

Lachlan woke up late and had a quiet morning playing on the computer. He pointed some words out on the spine of a DVD which were "Mickey Mouse Clubhouse" and then found a picture online of a USA flag. Next he pointed to the toolbar on the computer and gestured for me to type in the words on the DVD spine, "Mickey Mouse Clubhouse" plus "USA". He wanted to search online and he had found a way to express what he wanted, like he always does.

Lachlan likes to play computer games in different languages. I have always thought that he seemed to understand languages other than English. This is another mystery, but I think he has learned the languages through the computer.

Once when Lachlan's older sister Samantha's friend John came to visit, he spoke to Lachlan in Spanish and Lachlan understood him. John asked Lachlan in Spanish if he would like to come and play and Lachlan stood up to go with him. John asked Lachlan various questions in Spanish while they were playing, such as asking Lachlan to bring toys or books, and Lachlan understood. John had no doubt that Lachlan understood the requests in Spanish. John was amazed as were the rest of the family.

We had always suspected that Lachlan could understand languages other than English as sometimes he watches DVDs in other languages as well. He is just as happy to watch them in any other language. The same applies to computer games. It does not matter which language they are in.

Lachlan has a respite carer Pamela, who has been supporting him for five years. Lachlan is always very pleased to see her and the two of them have built up a lovely relationship over the years. It has been very helpful to have Pamela come and visit and play with

Lachlan while I go out for a couple of hours and of course Lachlan loves it too.

Pamela would often say that Lachlan was playing games in other languages, and sometimes we could not figure out which language it was. At first, I think Pamela was surprised about the languages but now she is used to Lachlan doing that. Pamela, I think, found this interesting and amusing.

This afternoon Lachlan went to a fair and drove a dodgem car. He absolutely loved the two-person car which suited him perfectly as Dad rode in it alongside him while he was driving it. Lachlan went on a swinging chair ride as well at the fair and the jumping castle and had the time of his life. These are things he would not have done when he was younger. He has changed a lot, especially since he has grown older and had Itsal as he is much less anxious about things. Lachlan mostly likes the same rides as other children his age and now has the freedom, through Itsal, to have these experiences.

Another time at Lachlan's cousin Steven's birthday party, Lachlan also wanted to drive a dodgem car. The dodgem cars at the birthday party (which were inside a bowling alley) only allowed one person to be inside the car so they were not really suitable for Lachlan. Lachlan needed to have another person in the car with him at least for the first time, in case he tried to stand up or exit the car. I feared that he would become injured should he stand up and get out of the car at the wrong time lest he be hit by another car. This time we had to say "No" to him riding in the dodgem car, but luckily there were plenty of other games for him to play so he did not seem to mind.

Wednesday 11/03/15

Today I bought Lachlan a small money box which locked with a small lock and key. I thought it would be good practice for his fine motor skills to practice opening and closing the money box lock. When Lachlan came home from school he played with the money box and seemed to like it. He went to my purse and I thought he was looking for some money to put into the money box, so I gave him some coins. He looked in the wallet section through the cards in there. He stopped when he came to the library card which reminded me that the DVDs that he had borrowed must have been due back soon. I looked for the email which would tell me when the DVDs were due back and which ones as I could not remember as there were over one hundred and eighty DVDs in Lachlan's collection and some from various local libraries. I realised that I must have accidently deleted the email I would have received from the library.

Lachlan nodded when I asked him if he wanted to go the library and I could tell he was excited about going there. He looked over his DVD collection and pulled a few of them out. I realised that he had pulled out the ones that were due back today. I have no idea how he knew they were due back today, as I did not know (given that I had lost the email from the library). Lachlan also remembered which ones were due back at each library and he knew which library cards each DVD was attached to. He would never make a mistake about something like that because his memory is so excellent. If he had needed to put them back in exactly the same location on the shelf from where he had retrieved them that would have been no problem at all. He would have easily remembered.

Monday 16/03/15

Today Lachlan is woken up with his DVD player as usual and when it was time for Itsal to encourage Lachlan to get out of bed, he came to see Lachlan with a Christmas tree sticker in his mouth which he must have found somewhere. Lachlan found this funny and laughed out loud when Itsal put it on his bed.

Sometimes Itsal will bring us a piece of paper or tissue which he has found because he remembers the time that I asked him to pick a piece of paper up so that it could be placed in the bin. So every now and then, Itsal brings us a little present like a sticker or piece of paper.

After school today Lachlan went out to the park to play and it must have been his lucky day as it rained twice at the park causing two rainbows to appear about twenty minutes apart. Lachlan was extremely excited as he has always loved rainbows.

When Lachlan was three years old, I remember showing him a rainbow which could be seen from our lounge room window once again. He was so excited and looked at it for a long time while opening and closing the blinds, making sure it would still be there when he opened the blinds again and he was so thrilled each time when he found that it was. He examined the rainbow from different angles which he often does when he looks at a subject he likes or finds interesting. He observed the rainbow from different windows and different angles from the same window. He opened and closed the blinds many times and watched the rainbow from different positions in the blinds.

The next morning when Lachlan woke up he ran to the window and opened the blinds looking for the rainbow. When he saw that it had disappeared, he pointed to the sky and I knew he was expecting me to put the rainbow back in the sky, the same as the day before. After I explained that rainbows did not stay in the sky and that they are only there for a short time he became quite upset and cried.

Then I thought of an idea, that perhaps Lachlan might like to paint a picture of a rainbow. So that is what we did, but not on the window, just on some paper. Lachlan has always loved to paint rainbows and still does, and he must paint them in the same colours as a rainbow song he knows. He started with red and painted the rainbow in the right order. He did a great job and he has many paintings and drawings of rainbows in his room which he started doing back in his preschool days.

Thursday 19/03/15

Today I drove Lachlan to school. It was a long drive for him (about an hour) which he would not have been able to cope with when he was younger. He would become upset when the lights turned red and we would have to stop, or when there was a lot of traffic and we had to stop and start often. These days he finds it a little boring perhaps but is used to the traffic lights and the car stopping and starting. He just watches all the traffic and I think he likes all the trucks and different vehicles he sees along the way. Lachlan has changed so much in this way as Itsal has helped Lachlan to feel more settled in the car. As soon as Itsal started travelling with Lachlan we noticed this change instantly!

In past years when we visited Lachlan's Nanna which involved a ninety minute car trip it was a real struggle for Lachlan to stay in the one spot for so long. It was especially bothersome for him on the way back being the second long car trip of the day. One way was enough as far as he was concerned! He would take his seatbelt off, jump up and down yelling and sometimes crying from boredom of it.

These days on very long trips Lachlan plays with some technology, listens to classical music or other songs he likes, and with Itsal in the car, he is a lot more settled than in the past. It is no problem going for a long drive anymore as long as Itsal in the car. In fact, Lachlan quite enjoys car trips these days. It was really different having a holiday with Itsal around. Lachlan just loves having his best friend go everywhere with him and Itsal seems to make him feel calm and happy.

After school, I picked Lachlan up and he seemed very happy to see me. He ate his muffin in the car on the way home and once home enjoyed a bit of down time playing a "Roary the Racing Car" game in German on the computer.

Next I found Lachlan putting my shoes on. They were black shoes with bows and as Lachlan's feet are almost the same size as mine, the shoes almost fitted him. He looked at his feet for a while with them on and seemed amused about this. He does not find this embarrassing and I am sure that even if we had visitors he would still wear my shoes. Perhaps he would ask the visitors for their shoes if he liked the look of them. He knows how to have fun and is not concerned about other people's opinions.

Friday 20/3/2015

Lachlan came home from school in a very happy mood. As usual he ate his afternoon tea, a muffin, and played with his DVD player. He was happy doing this for longer than usual before requesting a trip to go to the library with his iPad.

He came home very happy from the library with three DVDs and while watching them played with Itsal giving him bear hugs. Lachlan pointed to a particular spot on the coffee table but there was nothing in that spot. I know that this meant he wanted whatever was in that spot previously. This time he wanted the iPod.

We know this because around two years ago Lachlan would point to a spot on the coffee table, then a different spot on the coffee table and then a spot on the kitchen table and then the television table. We worked out that the item he was looking for was in the places he pointed to and probably in the same order as well. Eventually we figured out that the iPod was in those places and therefore must have been the item he was looking for.

How amazing that he remembered that the iPod was in one spot on the coffee table then a second spot on the coffee table, then a spot on the kitchen table, and then a spot on the television table. How cleverly he communicated his needs.

After the bedtime routine Lachlan brushed his teeth. He has just started to brush his teeth last thing before bed rather than at bath time, as this way we can be sure there would be no more eating or drinking for the night, keeping his teeth healthier. He has adjusted to the change in the routine quite well. Lachlan really is not keen on brushing his teeth as he is super sensitive, I would say that he perhaps finds it a little painful. When brushing we begin a count down from one hundred to one so that he knows that there is a starting point and an end point approaching. If Lachlan is in an unhappy mood I count down really fast.

Counting down works really well for Lachlan when starting something new or with an activity he does not like. When Lachlan was little, I used to count down with nail cutting by showing him large numbers which I had drawn on cardboard cards starting with ten and counting down to one until the last nail was done. These days I do not need to use the cards or count down when cutting Lachlan's nails as he is used to it now and does not seem to mind at all. In fact, when one of his nails has been chipped or broken or is too long, he comes and points it out to me and I know to trim it for him. See how he gets his message across without words!

Being Friday, Lachlan fell asleep quickly tonight. Tired as usual by the end of the school week.

Sunday 22/03/15

Today Lachlan came home from his outing walking like someone in a cowboy movie, (which I could relate to after horse riding). I wondered if he was sore, but he seemed fine and could still jump around as usual. Lachlan had been to the opening of a new equestrian centre. He was very tense while in the car on the way but once he arrived and was around the horses he seemed very calm and relaxed.

He had a ride on a horse and really enjoyed watching the show jumping outside. The people there were very friendly and spoke to him a lot, which he liked. Lachlan loves horses and all farm animals. Lachlan's grandfather was a farmer so maybe that is where it comes from. Horses and dogs seem to have this effect on him.

After visiting the equestrian centre Lachlan went to the airport with his Dad (who once had a pilot licence), so the two of them really enjoyed watching the planes today just as they do whenever they visit the airport. Today there was a really huge one there, an Airbus A380.

When we flew to Melbourne to Righteous Pups Australia to do the training for Lachlan's Assistance Dog, Lachlan was invited into the cockpit of the plane which he was extremely excited about. He started jumping up and down with excitement when he saw all the controls in the cockpit.

Monday 23/03/15

This morning Lachlan woke up around 4.30 a.m.
Sometimes this happens and we are not sure why.
Lachlan was in a happy mood, but Itsal knew that it was

too early for school and Lachlan does not ordinarily entertain himself unsupervised. Knowing this, Itsal came into my room and woke me to let me know that Lachlan was up. What a wonderful dog he is and what a huge relief to know that we have an extra helper who just seems to know what to do and when to do it. He notices instantly any change to Lachlan's usual routine.

When Lachlan returned from school he seemed tired. School told me that Lachlan had started in an additional reading group to maximise his potential, which he will do twice a week. He is very good at reading and spelling which I noticed when he was about two years old as he could read some words by pointing at them when asked. He could spell his name back then at age two and he would spell it out with foam letters. When asked how to spell 'Mum' and other words, he knew the answer and would use the foam letters to spell the words. Perhaps he had remembered seeing the words written somewhere.

This afternoon Lachlan started to cry without any warning. We did not notice any reason for the crying so we asked Lachlan to communicate with us on his iPad and we prompted him by pressing the two buttons "I" and "Feel" then asked him to press the next word in the phrase. He pressed "Sick" and then the iPad spoke out "I feel sick". How wonderful that he has this mode of communication! Being visual Lachlan responds to it extremely well. We are unsure why Lachlan felt sick, but after sitting quietly for about ten minutes it passed and Lachlan went back to his usual happy self.

This evening Lachlan watched a Thomas the Tank Engine movie which lasted one hour. He seemed to really enjoy it. This is a big improvement as in the past he would have found this too long, too boring and/or overwhelming. The big picture on the television screen as well as the noise would have been overstimulating for him. Lachlan likes to have control of the television remote as he likes to be able to switch over the channel should he find a program overwhelming. It is less overwhelming for him if the sound is muted. We have watched many a television show without sound for this reason. Not quite as good, but we are getting very good at lip reading!

Itsal seemed very concerned when he saw my reaction after I noticed some sort of insect in my hair after being outside. He came to investigate immediately to see if he could help, but in this case he couldn't.

Wednesday 25/03/15

Itsal helps to raise Lachlan from his bed this morning as usual, which is a godsend. This is one of main ways which Itsal helps Lachlan and myself. When Itsal is called in the morning, he knows exactly what to do. Rarely do I need to give a command for the morning routine, as Itsal knows how it all works and so does Lachlan. After jumping onto Lachlan's bed, Itsal looks for a gap where he can nudge or lick Lachlan's arm, a place which is not covered by clothing, a pillow or blankets.

At this point Itsal always reminds me that I need to move Lachlan's DVD player into the lounge room by putting his paw on the DVD player and nudging it in front of me, because there are times when I get busy talking to Lachlan and forget.

Itsal then nudges at the uncovered spot (usually one of Lachlan's arms), while Lachlan tosses and turns, until he finds another spot and then nudges in the new spot. Itsal nudges a few times which usually prompts Lachlan to sit up in bed, when Itsal takes the opportunity to sit on Lachlan's pillow preventing Lachlan from lying down again.

Sometimes Lachlan sits up for a few minutes and plays with Itsal, then gets out of bed. Having Itsal to help with this makes life so much easier. Without Itsal, I would need to convince Lachlan that although he is very sleepy, he needs to wake up, get dressed and go to school. With Itsal involved in the morning routine, Lachlan is so much happier and even when he is very tired he is still happy to see Itsal each morning. Lachlan understands that Itsal is a special friend who helps a lot, I think.

Friday 27/03/15

After a usual day at school, Lachlan had his afternoon tea and then it was time for an outing. Lachlan loves to go out in the afternoons and today I offered two options. The first option being the park (he loves the swings there), or option two: the shops to have a look around. We requested Lachlan type out his answer on the iPad, and to start this off, I wrote out two sentences on a piece of paper so that Lachlan could choose an option and then type it into the iPad program which would speak it out.

1. I want to go to the park to play
2. I want to go to the shops

I asked Lachlan to choose what he would like to do and type it out but he clearly had something else in mind. He quickly went to his PECS folder so that he could let me know what it was. He looked in his folder and arranged a sentence to show me. He found the PECS pictures that he was looking for and then he gestured for me to come and look at his folder.

He wanted to go to the shops and buy a DVD, he had selected "Toys R Us" making sure that I knew his preferred shop to visit. Well, this was a good motivator for him to type requests out on the iPad, I thought to myself. We are hoping that Lachlan will learn to type out all of his requests in the future, so I wrote the sentence out on a piece of paper, "I want to go to Toys R Us and buy a DVD". Lachlan knew that I wanted him to type this out so he looked at the sentence and copied it onto the iPad. He pressed the speak button and heard the sentence aloud. How wonderful that he has a voice!

It is very exciting that Lachlan has this means for his voice to be heard and that he can talk to us in this way. As well as requests, he can express feelings too and I am very grateful that he was born at a time when this type of communication is available to him especially at an age when he has the ability to use it to communicate all his wants and needs.

Off we go to the shops to buy a DVD with Itsal. It is so much easier taking Lachlan out now that we have Itsal. Lachlan is a lot less concerned about most things at the shops these days. He is a not overwhelmed anymore. He does not find it all too much. Even when the shops are crowded Lachlan keeps his attention focused on Itsal (and DVDs) and things that have worried him in the past do not seem to concern him anymore. Itsal has a calming effect on Lachlan and all of us overall, but I notice the difference especially when taking Lachlan out between a distressing outing and an enjoyable one.

During the evening Lachlan watched YouTube videos. When he found some he really liked he gestured for me to come and have a look and put his arm around my neck, keeping me close so that I would see the exciting YouTube clips he had found. This is also a new behaviour as the idea of him pointing out something he liked or sharing something with someone else would not have occurred to him when he was younger. People matter a lot more now to him than they used to and I can see that Lachlan's autism is fading as he gets older.

Tuesday 31/03/15

While Lachlan played on the computer this afternoon he typed into the toolbar 'La maison de Mickey' and as I did not know what that meant, I waited to see what would come up on the computer. Various YouTube episodes of Mickey Mouse appeared in French and Lachlan seemed to know which ones he was looking for. When I typed 'La maison de Mickey' into Google to translate I found out that this meant 'The house of Mickey'.

It seemed that Lachlan had been learning to understand French (and other languages) and could also remember how to type the words as well. How and why? Lachlan has always been interested in watching television shows in languages other than English and I have wondered what his motivation was to do it and I still do not know. As far as Lachlan is concerned, it is just as good in any other language as it is in English.

We have now discovered another talent of his and wonder how many languages he could learn if he wanted to. He has an excellent memory. Should we decide to take Lachlan to Europe this skill will come in very handy for everyone.

Lachlan loves flying in planes and has travelled to America and Thailand. It worked out best to travel on overnight flights so that he could sleep most of the time he was on the plane. This helped alleviate the boredom and sitting for long periods of time. It had worked out fine when he woke up in the morning with still two or three hours of flying time left. He was able to manage sitting for a few hours.

When we went to Thailand we took most of the same snacks that Lachlan was eating at home at that point in time as we thought it unlikely the same ones would be available in Thailand. We did this when we travelled to America as well. We found similar products in America but Lachlan will only eat things exactly the same as the ones he is used to. The chef at the restaurant where we stayed called Lachlan "Mr Peanut" (which Lachlan thought was funny) and each night he would bring Lachlan a plate with some peanut butter and bread rolls as Lachlan did not want to eat any other food from the restaurant, except on two occasions when he ate small chocolate chip muffins.

Since then, we realised that wherever we stay needs to have a kitchen or at least a kitchenette with a microwave, stove and fridge so that Lachlan's foods can be made the same as at home as Lachlan does not eat take-away food or food from restaurants. When we went to America Lachlan needed to change the juice he drank as they did not have the same juice over there, (at least at the shop nearby), which was apple and blackcurrant. He chose cherry juice and drank that diluted with water as it was the same colour as apple and blackcurrant juice which was the only drink he drank at the time. The trick is to try and keep as many things as possible the same as at home when going on holiday. That is what works for Lachlan.

Chapter 4
April 2015

Wednesday 01/04/15

Today Lachlan came home from school wearing his Spiderman outfit as there had been a dress up party at school. Strangely enough when I asked him to try it on yesterday to see how it would fit, he seemed unhappy that it was a little tight and wanted to take it off straight away. However, he was happy to wear it to the party at school and joined in with all the other children dressing up and having fun.

This evening Lachlan studied his DVD collection for some time before he pointed to some writing on the spine of a DVD and gestured for me to type the words into the toolbar. He wanted to investigate other possible DVDs made by the same manufacturer. Thinking it would be best for his independence, I asked him to type the words himself so he studied the letters before he typed them into the toolbar.

Thursday 02/04/15

Today was last day of the term and being Mufti Day, the children did not have to wear their school uniforms. Lachlan had never participated in Mufti Day before as I thought he may not have liked the change to his usual morning routine by not wearing his uniform. Today I thought it was time to try it out so I made a social story on the iPad which said, "Today is Mufti day and I can wear anything I want to school". I pressed the 'speak' button and Lachlan nodded indicating that he understood. Next I asked him to choose the clothes he wanted to wear and showed him some options. He chose a green T-shirt and some black shorts. Lachlan happily joined the others in the school bus wearing his Mufti clothes and an Easter hat which his sister Samantha had made. The Easter hat looked like a bird nest on his head as the hat could hardly be seen. Lachlan loved it.

Lachlan has come a long way from when he first started catching the bus to school a year ago. Last year he had a most unusual habit whereby each day on the way out to get into the school bus he would stop on the verandah and touch each and every panel on the side of the house. Lachlan would insist on doing this every day and would not enter the bus without having touched each panel first. When Lachlan first started doing this I thought he was counting the panels so I assured him the same amount of panels would be there the next day and therefore he did not need to count them again. He still continued to do it so I counted aloud as he touched the panels and hoped he would agree that he did not need to repeat this each day. Eventually I realised that this was a ritual that Lachlan had, and it was not about counting. The ritual was to touch each panel on the way to the bus. So be it. Lachlan liked it and it did not hurt anyone, so I never mentioned it again. Some weeks later he stopped touching the panels. I am not sure why he started touching the panels or why he stopped touching them. One year down the track Lachlan loves the bus ride and enjoys going to school and could not be happier with the morning routine.

Lachlan also used to find stopping at traffic lights frustrating. We would have to limit car travel time to around an hour at which time Lachlan would begin losing patience. It was hard for him to visit his grandparents because the drive to their house took too long. These days with Itsal in the car Lachlan is able to sit for a few hours without any frustration. He actually enjoys car travel! Last year we took Lachlan on a holiday to NSW North Coast which was his first long car trip and for the first time he was not frustrated by it. Thank you Itsal!

Good Friday 03/04/15

We went to visit relatives today. As usual Lachlan was interested in Uncle Jim's beard and as usual Uncle Jim found this amusing and told us that many children were interested in his beard and liked to feel it. He told us that Lachlan liked to grab onto his beard and pull it really hard. Ouch! Uncle Jim still found this funny, as did Lachlan's cousin Daniel, who Lachlan often grabs in a headlock.

Lachlan did not intend to hurt anyone he wanted to explore the texture of the beard just as he had done with the wooden house panels. He wanted to repeat the feeling, perhaps to see if it remained the same each and every time over a span of months. If he found it did he would no longer need to repeat the experience and might stop.

Daniel commented about how strong Lachlan was and having been caught in Lachlan's headlock a few times myself, I had to agree. Lachlan does seem to be incredibly strong as well as big for his age.

Of course Itsal was a big hit with all family members. Everyone wanted to know exactly what he did and hear about the many ways he helped. In the meantime Lachlan walked along ledges of the retaining walls outside as his two uncles kept their eyes on him. As he walked along the ledges the drop became higher and higher increasing his risk of injury should he have lost his balance and fallen. His uncles noticed how finely he balanced his body, but still watched him cautiously which allowed me to chat to other family members.

When I saw Lachlan balancing on the ledges I had no doubt that he would be safe as I had seen him do this sort of thing many times before. Lachlan has no fear of accidents, but knows exactly what he is capable of and he rarely misjudges his movements.

Saturday 04/04/15

At breakfast time Lachlan watched Mickey Mouse in Spanish a number of times. Afterwards we went to a large shopping plaza. Even though this was Lachlan's first time at this particular shopping centre he was not stressed at all. This was unbelievable! It has taken just one year of having Itsal for the problem of shopping centre stress to be completely resolved. Before Itsal came along, going to an unfamiliar shopping centre would not have been possible for Lachlan as he had always found shopping centres far too overwhelming with the crowds and noise.

Lachlan was quite excited to be at the shopping centre today. He looked into the centre structure of the plaza to find rides and shops he was interested in. We explained to Lachlan that we needed to go down two floors to get to the place he was interested in visiting. We were sure he would remember those directions should he ever go back to the same shopping plaza. While looking in the shops Lachlan found and chose an elf costume which he needed to buy for an upcoming school party.

Easter Sunday 05/04/15

I woke up at 2.30 a.m. as I heard Lachlan vocalising in his room. As Itsal had not woken me, I knew there was nothing of great concern occurring in Lachlan's room at the time. When I went into his room, I had the sense that he was still half asleep and perhaps had woken due to a dream. Lachlan wanted to hold my hand and he tucked it right under his chest and laid on it and drifted back to sleep. Now I needed to plan my getaway so I waited for fifteen minutes until Lachlan was fast asleep before slowly and carefully removing my hand. He did not stir and slept until light.

When Lachlan woke again, I reminded him that it was Easter Sunday and that the Easter Bunny might have left him a present. On hearing this, he quickly jumped out of bed to investigate. He found some Easter eggs but was not impressed by those and he looked around to see if there were any presents that he would like. Luckily the Easter Bunny knew that Lachlan was not very interested in Easter eggs so had left another present, a DVD.

Lachlan does not usually eat Easter eggs or chocolates but has a few times in the past. However, he does like to eat a chocolate biscuit every now and then. We never know if he will change his mind and start eating Easter eggs again, but not today. He was much more interested in the DVD.

Lachlan found and watched various YouTube video cartoons in Spanish, and found one in English where there was a man singing songs using sign language. Lachlan was very excited to have discovered this cartoon and came to the kitchen to relay his excitement to me. Lachlan knows many hand signs. The one on the YouTube clip one was in Auslan.

This afternoon Lachlan visited the Easter show. At first Lachlan wanted to find a corner to stay in to shield himself from the people, noises and movement, colour and busyness. He stayed in the corner for around fifteen minutes to observe what was happening around him. He passed a circus tent and was curious to take a look inside. He seemed very interested and walked onto the stage and looked around at all the equipment there. He was especially interested in a seesaw and some mats.

When asked if he wanted to see the show he nodded in agreement so we went and bought tickets as we could see the show was about to begin. Lachlan was very excited when the show started. He looked up at a performer who was doing tricks on high wire rings and Lachlan started to dance to the music that played. Lachlan stood up in his seat throughout the different performances, and danced when he liked the music. He enjoyed both the music and performances equally.

After the circus, Lachlan looked around at the rides and decided to have a turn on a giant slide. He waited his turn and had five turns in total. Next he had turns on two different merry-go-rounds. After walking around and looking at various things, Lachlan found a quiet spot near some large trees where he wanted to stay as he enjoyed hopping on and off some large paving stones. After giving himself some time out Lachlan wanted to go back to the rides and was particularly interested in watching the pirate ship.

Lachlan went on the tea cup ride. He loved the way it spun around, and he did not become sick from spinning. When he was preschool age he would often want to be spun around on a swivel chair. It would make him dizzy but he still wanted to keep spinning as he enjoyed the sensation. Lachlan also enjoys watching spinning objects, like fans or car wheels or his mother.

As Lachlan's level of anxiety reduced, he has been able to visit many different and unfamiliar shopping centres over the past year. Due to Itsal's calming effect, Lachlan has become better used to the sensory overload of shopping centres and he is a lot less stressed and able cope with the overload. We are totally amazed that only one year later Lachlan can go to any shopping centre and he actually enjoys it. He will now ride on children's rides which is another new activity he now is now able to enjoy.

Tuesday 07/04/15

Lachlan went to the movies this afternoon to see the SpongeBob Square Pants movie. He has been to the movies on two other occasions and on both had found it too overstimulating and wanted to leave after five or ten minutes. Lachlan had shown some interest in watching this particular movie after he saw an advertisement about it on the computer and pointed it out to me. Perhaps it was time to give the movies another try, I thought.

We went with Jo (Lachlan's aunt) and cousins, Billy and Steven. When we arrived at the movies Lachlan was hesitant to go inside and stopped outside with Itsal and watched people going in and out of the entrance. After I reassured him that there was fun to be had, I asked him if he wanted to have a turn on the game machines inside. He decided to go inside and after he had a good look at all the games, he chose a car to ride on. Lachlan had some turns on the car ride while we waited for the others to return from the queue with the tickets.

Lachlan held his ticket while we headed to the correct door. Itsal seemed at home at the movies and I was sure he had been before. On the way through the corridor to the movie doors, the security guard stopped us and asked about Itsal making sure he was an assistance dog. I asked the security guard if he wanted to see Itsal's licence but he said it was not necessary. Once inside, we found a seat at the side of the front row. In this corner there were no other people in Lachlan's view front or back which I thought would be best. Lachlan sat next to myself while Jo, Billy and Steven sat in the row opposite us. There were only a few people inside the cinema which worked out very well for Lachlan making it quieter. The less people the better as far as Lachlan was concerned. He liked the quiet space in the corner away from other people.

Lachlan was so excited when the movie started. Sometimes he would stand up and jump up and down and then he sat for a while and watched the movie while he ate his bread rolls. Lachlan does not eat popcorn or foods available at the movies. Every now and then while he watched the movie he would give me a hug and tap me on the head. When Lachlan taps people on the head it is almost like he is saying "hello", "I'm glad you are here", or "look at me". It is a good and positive sign which means he is happy. Lachlan also danced at times during the movie when music played.

After a while I noticed that this was the longest period of time he had ever stayed in the cinema and I wondered whether he would want to stay for the whole movie. As it worked out he did. Thank you Itsal! How exciting for Lachlan to have watched a whole movie for the first time in a cinema. This was a huge step for him and I think that having Itsal with him today gave him the confidence to go ahead. I am sure Lachlan would not have entered the cinema today without Itsal. For Lachlan, it was like holding his best friend's hand.

Lachlan watched the film credits and did not want to leave until he saw the very last one. I noticed that there was only one other person left in the cinema but Lachlan did not want to leave while any part of the film credits were still showing. Aunty Jo came to remind him that the movie had finished and it was now time to leave. Lachlan listened to her because Aunty Jo is not his Mum and also because he likes her a lot.

Thursday 09/04/15

Today Lachlan had a dental appointment. We had been practising dental examinations at home using a fake plastic mirror given to Lachlan by the dentist at his last visit. Last time he was willing to sit in the chair and open his mouth long enough to allow the dentist to have a quick examination. This time Lachlan was much more willing to be examined especially when the dentist gave me the mirror to place of inside Lachlan's mouth and she just looked while I held it. He was comfortable with this technique which allowed the dentist to examine his top and bottom teeth. We were told that two of the teeth needed some investigation/work for which Lachlan would need to be sedated.

Lachlan has come a long way with dental visits. At his first visit he was willing to sit in the chair for only a few minutes and opened his mouth several times but allowed only a very brief examination. These days he allows a longer examination and he is used to flossing and brushing which we do each evening. Not one of

Lachlan's favourite things, but he has learned to tolerate it. He knows it is important.

Friday 10/04/15

Lachlan was not feeling very well today and I wondered if he was coming down with a cold. He had a sniffle throughout the night and today his nose looked very inflamed, perhaps from rubbing. I told him that we needed to go and see the doctor who may prescribe some ointment for his nose. He nodded in agreement which suggested his nose must have been quite sore.

As the morning progressed and we prepared to go out I noticed that Lachlan had very little to drink and had not eaten his breakfast. I usually wait until Lachlan has eaten his breakfast before we go out, but sometimes this can take a long time so there are times when we need to put his breakfast in a plastic bag and take it out with us. Luckily he usually has toast for breakfast so we can do this if necessary. Lucky for me, he does not eat cereal for breakfast.

While I waited to see whether Lachlan would eat and drink before we went out, I got busy with the household task of making the bed. Lachlan came over and placed a container of my facial moisturiser on the bed. When I asked him what he was doing, he pointed to his nose. He was hoping that the moisturising cream may have helped. After I told him that this type of cream probably would not help he suggested, by pointing, to another type of skin cream which was sitting on my dressing table. Not knowing whether these creams would sting Lachlan's face, I did not want to use them on him. It seemed as though Lachlan really wanted some ointment for his face, so we planned go to the pharmacy to buy some to use until the doctor's rooms reopened that afternoon.

We went to the pharmacy to buy some ointment and also to the library which was close by. Lachlan walked straight over to the general section and picked up a DVD about pirates. He seemed to know exactly where it would be without looking at the others on the shelf, so I guess he must have remembered the location from a previous visit.

Lachlan seemed happier after we applied the ointment, knowing it would help his sore nose along until we could see the doctor later that afternoon. Pamela, Lachlan's respite carer was due to arrive. She would look after Lachlan for two hours. When Pamela arrived Lachlan seemed very pleased to see her and he approached her immediately. Pamela noticed how much bigger Lachlan looked since she had last seen him. Lachlan approached Pamela again and the two of them started dancing which meant it was time for me to go to my hair appointment (I knew I would not be missed).

That afternoon the doctor found that Lachlan had an allergy, not a cold like I had thought. He gave us a script for some allergy medication which he said could be disguised in a drink if necessary as Lachlan would not drink strong tasting medicine. The doctor was right and Lachlan did not notice the medication in his drink at all. He drank all of it along with some paracetamol and then went to bed for the night. The medications worked like a charm and Lachlan slept well overnight.

Saturday 11/04/15

Lachlan seemed much better today and rested at home for the day.

Monday 13/04/15

As Lachlan seemed well again, today we went to an amusement park. Lachlan had often pointed it out on his way to other places which indicated his interest. Again we went with Lachlan's Aunty Jo, and cousins Billy (14), and Steven who is 8 years old also (six months older than Lachlan), Samantha (Lachlan's sister, who is 25) and myself and Itsal of course. Lachlan was very excited when arrived at the entry gate. There was a big Ferris wheel and the three boys and Samantha were all very interested in having a ride. We decided not to put Itsal on the ride, even though he would have been allowed. We thought that four people as well as a dog might be too many, so Itsal stayed with Jo and myself while Lachlan, Samantha, Billy and Steven joined the ride. I noticed that as the ride took off Lachlan was standing and Samantha was doing her best to encourage him to sit down. Lachlan was so excited that he jumped up and down as the Ferris wheel rose up higher and higher. At times while the ride was moving Lachlan sat down next to Billy and at other times he sat next to Samantha on the opposite side. We waved to them and Steven waved back, but Lachlan did not notice us as he was too busy jumping up and down and having fun.

Itsal stared at the Ferris wheel carriages with great concern. He looked very alert and was ready to spring into action. He did not move or even look away until the ride stopped and the riders started to exit. He watched carefully to make sure Lachlan, Samantha, Billy and Steven were going to come off the Ferris wheel. When the first carriage stopped for riders to exit and Lachlan did not come out, Itsal fixed his attention on the rest of the carriages. He was so fixated on the carriages that when I called him he did not even turn around. Itsal wanted to see Lachlan come out of the ride and he looked so relieved when he finally saw him. In hindsight, it may have been better for Itsal to have gone on the Ferris wheel with Lachlan as he seemed so worried. I thought Itsal may have made the carriage too crowded but think Itsal would have preferred to ride with Lachlan, having seen his reaction today.

When everyone had finished their ride on the Ferris wheel, Steven told me that inside the ride there was a sign which said, 'No standing, rocking the carriage or jumping', (or words to that effect). Steven and Billy told us that Lachlan had been doing all three things, especially jumping. Billy told us that Steven pointed out the sign to Lachlan and asked him to, "Please read it". Lachlan just kept on jumping as he was not frightened at all. Lachlan thought it was fun! Steven seemed to be a little disturbed that Lachlan was not doing as the sign said he should. Poor Steven had wanted everyone to do the right thing and follow the sign. Samantha and Billy were just laughing while Lachlan was jumping and rocking the carriage, poor Steven was a little scared.

After the Ferris wheel ride Steven asked me if Lachlan was able to read the sign and I confirmed that he could. Next Steven queried that if Lachlan was able to read the sign, why did he not do as the sign asked. I told him that I did not know. Everyone was amused, but more by Steven's questions than by Lachlan's reaction.

Lachlan wanted to go on the Ferris wheel a second time, but I noticed Steven and the others were not so keen. Lachlan became interested in some side shows and the merry-go-round and forgot about the Ferris wheel. Jo, Lachlan, Itsal and myself had a ride on a merry-go-round. I wondered if Itsal had been on one before as he carefully climbed the small stairs to get onto merry-go-round, perhaps for the first time. He did not seem to mind riding on the merry-go-round and Lachlan was delighted. Lachlan loves anything that spins around.

Next Lachlan played some side-show games and won two small toys. Next he wanted to have a turn on dodgem cars so he waited in the queue as long as he could but found the noise from the waiting crowd challenging and needed to have a short break outside. When we went back to re-join the queue, the others in the family were at the front and as they opened the gate Lachlan joined Samantha in a dodgem car. As I watched them ride around, their car was bumped a number of times by other cars which Lachlan seemed to enjoy.

After the dodgem car ride Samantha took Lachlan into a maze while Itsal and I waited outside. When Lachlan and Samantha came out a short time later, Lachlan was ready to go home. He seemed tired and signed the "Finished" sign a number of times. I told Lachlan that we would go home as soon as the others had been on the rides they wanted. Lachlan was a little unhappy about waiting for the others who had spread out and were all on different rides, so he sat down on a step next to Itsal. Lachlan started to cry as he just wanted to go home. We needed to wait until the others returned to ask them how long they wished to stay and then figure out the best thing to do after that.

While we waited Lachlan was quite upset which I thought was unusual. I think he had become tired and I noticed that the amusement park had become more crowded and noisy. I talked to him and tried to cheer him up but he really did not like waiting at all. While we sat and waited a young woman approached us and asked about Itsal. She wanted to know whose assistance dog

Itsal was. I told her that Itsal was Lachlan's dog and then told her that it was difficult for me to chat as Lachlan was clearly very upset. She told me that she understood and that she was one of eight children and that five of her siblings had a disability. She told me her name was Tara and told me that her siblings had autism, cerebral palsy, a brain injury and an intellectual disability.

Tara began talking to Lachlan. She asked him questions about Itsal and himself and I noticed that Lachlan seemed to be listening to her and he had slowly calmed down. Tara asked me if she could give Lachlan a present to which I replied, "No thanks" but then she pulled a rainbow coloured spring out of her pocket and opened it. Lachlan liked it and she insisted that he kept it. It did seem to calm him even more as he was distracted from waiting while he played with it. Lachlan signed the "Thank you" sign to thank Tara. Tara then bought her fiancé over to meet Lachlan and I, as well as Samantha who had now returned, and then Tara and her fiancé left. What a lovely thoughtful woman we all thought she was.

Steven had one last ride and then we all headed home. Perhaps Lachlan was still slightly unwell which would have explained why he had been so upset during the afternoon.

Tuesday 15/04/15

Lachlan had a much quieter day today. He was happy watching DVDs and playing computer games. He asked to go to the library so I asked him to find the DVDs that we needed to take back. While I was getting ready to go Lachlan gathered together a pile of DVDs. Lachlan nodded when I asked him if he was sure the DVDs he had piled together were the right ones, (which was helpful as I could not remember which ones he chose last time). Lachlan never makes a mistake about DVDs so I assumed they must have been the right ones and when I checked the receipt I found he was right.

At the library Lachlan placed the DVDs being returned in the correct slot at the counter. After he chose more DVDs he took them to the scanning counter and then put them into the machine which opened the cases. Lachlan is well known at this particular local library and also at some of the other libraries. He signed "Thank you" to the librarian and happily left with the DVDs.

Wednesday 16/04/15

Itsal woke me at 6.00 a.m. this morning and then I noticed the light had been switched on in Lachlan's room. Lachlan must have been up and out of bed. Itsal did a great job by alerting me that Lachlan was awake. It worked out well that Lachlan had woken early because we were able to get organised for the day and go out earlier. Today we went to visit a farm with Aunty Jo, Billy and Steven. Lachlan liked looking at all the animals but was not particularly interested in feeding them today although he liked watching me feed them.

There was a particular kangaroo which Lachlan liked a lot which went back to pat several times. The kangaroo did not seem to mind that Lachlan was being slightly rough; it did not even try to move away.

Lachlan was often scared of animals when he was younger, but these days he likes them, especially farm animals. He liked the fluffy chickens and different coloured rabbits at the farm. He signed the correct hand signs for the animals when he saw them. He signed "sheep", "chicken", "cow", "pig" and "dog". When we saw the rabbits Lachlan watched to see how I signed for 'rabbit' so that he could do the same. I was unsure what the sign for 'rabbit' was, so I made one up which was the best I could do. I wondered what would happen when I found out the correct sign for 'rabbit' and showed it to Lachlan. Would he remember the first wrong one I had shown him and then think the right one was wrong?

Lachlan loved watching the working dogs round up sheep and when I asked him if he enjoyed the working dog show he answered by saying "Yes". It is rare but sometimes Lachlan speaks. At times he says, "I do" when he wants to do a task independently and does not want my help. "I do" means; I will do it, not you. Sometimes Lachlan also says, "I do" when he is asked a question about something he likes. It is very exciting for us when he answers.

Friday 17/04/15

This morning Pamela (Lachlan's respite carer), came over to our house to play with Lachlan for a couple of hours. Lachlan was busy watching his DVDs and still in bed so he continued with that, as I left to go out. Lachlan was very pleased to stay with Pamela.

When I returned from my outing, Pamela told me that Lachlan had found something he wanted to buy on the internet and asked her for her credit card and I knew exactly what she had meant. It was probably an app he liked as he has often found them and pointed them out before gesturing to me to put in my credit card number. If he is lucky the answer is yes.

This afternoon Lachlan played in the backyard spa as it was very warm outside. He put his surfboard in the water to practice. He sat and laid on it and tried all sorts of moves. He had a fantastic time practicing on his surfboard.

Sunday 19/04/15

We needed to go and buy some drinks for Lachlan. He drinks just one type of juice only which until recently had been available at major local supermarkets. When we rang the supplier they told us these drinks were available at a smaller supermarket chain, however, we found that only some of the stores stocked the drinks. Some of the stores were willing to order them in for us, which was helpful but we found that sometimes the drinks were available and at other times they were not. We tried all stores within roughly a twenty-kilometre radius from home.

We found out that two stores closest to home would soon not be stocking the drinks, so we would need to go to an out-of-area store. We bought a big supply of drinks today and the store promised to phone when the next order of drinks arrived. Sounds like a very good time for Lachlan to switch to another type of drink!

At the supermarket today I checked all the drinks and tried to find one which was a similar colour and flavour to the current one as I had learned from Debbie (speech therapist) that Lachlan would be more likely to accept drinks of a similar colour and flavour to his current ones.

After managing to find a similar drink, I was pleasantly surprised when Lachlan accepted it when I added it to his usual drink bottle. It was less sweet and slightly darker in colour than the one he was used to so I was surprised when he tried it and drank quite a lot of it. What a huge breakthrough!

We now know which drinks to buy when the current supply dries up and it will also be much easier being able to buy drinks from the local supermarkets instead of driving around to different shops and areas to buy the drinks. Yippee!

Debbie has taught us that to change things we must start with something close to what Lachlan already eats and drinks. The same colour, texture and similar taste. This really worked for Lachlan in changing the drink today. This is a great news for us. Thanks Debbie!

Monday 20/04/15

Today is the last day of the school holidays. Samantha came to visit and spent time with Lachlan, while I attended an appointment. Thank you Samantha! Samantha and Lachlan put together an air hockey table while I was away. Lachlan helped with sawing the wood and screwing in some of the screws. Lachlan enjoyed building the table as he has an interest in building and construction.

Tuesday 21/04/15

It was the first school day of term two and Itsal knew exactly what to do. He joined in on the morning routine and nudged Lachlan's arms to help wake him up. Next Itsal jumped onto Lachlan's bed and sat down. Lachlan turned around and patted him for a while and then pushed him off the bed. Lachlan was now awake and watched a DVD until it was time for him to get dressed in his school uniform. Itsal jumped back onto the bed and sat on Lachlan's pillow, which meant that Lachlan needed to sit up because he could not lie back down. Lachlan got out of bed and Itsal waited for approval that his job was done. Fantastic work Itsal!

Lachlan was very excited to go back to school today. For the first time I did not use a social story to count down the days until school went back. Instead, yesterday I explained to Lachlan that tomorrow he would go back to school. I asked him if he was looking forward to seeing his friends and he nodded. It seems that Lachlan does not need the social story for going back to school anymore. He understands that holidays end and he has to go back to school. In fact, he was so excited that he wanted to wait on the verandah for the school bus to come, instead of staying inside and watching his DVDs as usual. It was extremely wet and cold outside today but Lachlan did not mind as he wanted to see the bus arrive. The school bus arrived fifteen minutes later than usual but Lachlan had waited for it happily. Inside the bus, I noticed a new travel assistant, but Lachlan was not bothered by the change.

The morning routine went smoothly and what a difference from when Lachlan first started school! These days he copes with changes to his routine provided the changes have been explained to him.

Sunday 26/04/15

Today Itsal woke me by standing next to me while I slept. He did not touch me but as he was rather close to my face, I woke up. Itsal had his toy seal in his mouth (one of the toys Lachlan won at the amusement park) which he seemed to have adopted as his own baby, as he takes it everywhere. Itsal had woken me as Lachlan was awake in his room watching a DVD.

As soon as I entered Lachlan's room, he signed the "Finished" sign as he saw me. This meant leave me alone, goodbye, I am busy with my DVD so come back later, that sort of thing. I no longer take this personally as I know Lachlan just wants to do his own thing. Lachlan likes to do this on the weekend especially, as during the week there are time limits on DVD watching in the mornings.

Samantha and her friend came over for a quick visit and Lachlan also signed the "Finished" sign when he saw them just in case they were thinking of asking him to do something, or perhaps because attention would have been directed to them instead of himself while they were visiting.

When Lachlan went to the shops this morning he saw a children's ride he was interested in. He wanted to go to different floors and observe the ride from various perspectives. Lachlan often does this and I think he finds it interesting that on a different floor, he can see the ride in another way. Sometimes he studies toys from various angles as well.

This afternoon Itsal started barking (which is unusual, as he rarely barks). When I went to the front door and opened it, nobody was there. Itsal sometimes barks when a car arrives at a house in the neighbourhood, particularly an unfamiliar one. He seems to know which cars are usually in the neighbourhood and if there is a different around, he lets us know. When I looked outside Itsal took my wrist in his mouth and led me away from the door and back to the kitchen where I'd been cooking busily until he had started barking. I was not sure what this meant but I guess he sensed that all was well and led me back to where I came from!

This evening Lachlan accepted and held onto a cheese stick which I had offered to him. It was not expected that he would eat it but just having it around or touching it would be a step towards eating it in the future. After he had held onto it for some time he began to shred it. I had left the room for a while and when I returned I noticed Lachlan had shredded more of the cheese. It also looked as though some of the cheese stick was missing, and I thought Lachlan might have eaten some. Or could Itsal have eaten it? I did not know for sure but assumed that if Itsal had eaten it he would have eaten the whole lot. Knowing that Itsal does not usually eat unless he has not been instructed to do so I thought it more likely that Lachlan did eat some of the cheese which was fantastic!

This evening Lachlan took himself into his room so that his evening routine could begin. This was unusual as he often does not want to go to bed. Lately he has been listening to audio books as part of his evening wind down. He really seems to enjoy them, especially the one about pirates which seems to have fascinated him lately.

Monday 27/04/15

Early this morning after Lachlan went to school I heard a crashing sound coming from the front room, which also started Itsal barking. After investigating I found one of Lachlan's DVD towers had fallen over. There are five towers of DVDs. The first one contained twenty-eight, the second eighty-nine, the third one had twenty-nine, then a tower of thirty-two and the last one had thirty-one. The largest tower of eighty-nine DVDs was the one which had fallen. This tower covered part of the television screen and for some reason Lachlan likes them to stay in the same order. One tower is so much bigger than the rest and no one knows why but Lachlan likes them this way. He knows if any have been moved around and he can tell if a tower falls during the day while he is at school as when he sees them, some are bound to be in the wrong order as I cannot remember their order in the same way that Lachlan does.

When Lachlan returned from school, and while I was busy making afternoon tea for him, I heard the DVD tower crash again. I did not know if they had fallen or whether Lachlan knocked them over on purpose, perhaps because I had put them back in the wrong order this morning. Lachlan asked for help by signing the "Help" sign. I picked up some of the DVDs and placed them back in the tower, but as I was unsure of the right order I placed three back at a time and Lachlan adjusted those three within the pile and placed them in their right positions as he remembered them before he moved on to the next three.

After a while Lachlan started rearranging the tower by himself and did not ask for my help. I guess he had figured out I did not know the order of the DVDs and that he was the best one to do it. I wondered what he thought about me not being able to recall the positions of the DVDs the way he did. I think he realises that no one else remembers the order of the DVDs.

This evening Lachlan listened to music in his room and we danced around which he loves to do. Sometimes he will repeat songs or parts of songs on a CD and of course he remembers the position of each song on every CD and exactly where all the parts are that he likes.

As Lachlan lay in bed and waited to fall asleep, he held my hand and this time he tucked it right under his chest, lay face down on it and turned around. I laughed to myself when I realised the predicament my body was in as my arm and my back were twisted. Lachlan was unable to see me as he has taken my hand and turned around and now faced the other way. I wondered how long I would be able to hold that position and knew I could not have kept it up for very long, ouch. After a few minutes Lachlan turned around, he still held my hand but lay flat on his back which was much better for me as no twisting was required!

There has always been a chair in Lachlan's room for this reason. It must be a quiet non-squeaky chair to allow a quiet escape when Lachlan has fallen off to sleep.

Tuesday 28/04/15

Itsal woke me this morning while it was still dark. He put his face near mine and made a soft whimpering sound. About one minute later Lachlan ran in and jumped onto the bed. Itsal knew that Lachlan needed me to be up once Lachlan had woken, especially since he was out of bed and moving around the house. What an amazing dog Itsal is! He knows what he needs to do without being instructed.

Lachlan was in a happy mood when he went to school even though he had woken up very early. When he was younger he would become upset if he woke up without an alarm as after watching DVDs he would realise that it was a school day. Lachlan would become upset when it was time to get dressed for school. These days he is aware of days of the week and knows which days are school days. He also loves going to school, which makes life much happier for him and all of us. Of course weekends are his favourite days.

This evening Lachlan listened to music in his room and because he was very happy and excited he tapped me on the head occasionally. It seems to be a way Lachlan expresses excitement and it can also be a request for deep pressure. This is a little quirky and funny and sometimes it hurts a little when he taps harder and catches me by surprise. After Lachlan tapped my head a few times, I softly tapped him back which made him laugh. He signed for "more" and we began a game taking turns of tapping each other. After we had played the tapping game for some time I asked him if he wanted to continue and he answered by saying "Yes". Lachlan does not speak very often but every now and then he says a word which is always very exciting for us. We always want to know what he is thinking.

Lachlan likes the head tapping game as he likes the feeling of pressure on his head. He also likes the feeling of deep pressure on his body and often gives family members big squeezes because he wants one. It seems that when he taps me on my head he would like to receive the same.

When Lachlan was younger he would often ask for squeezes when we were out shopping by giving me a big hug, which meant he wanted a big hug and squeeze back. Head tapping would probably look rather odd in public unless it was done between children as it would then go unnoticed. Lachlan does not seem to do any head tapping when out in public, only hugging. Lucky!

Thursday 30/04/15

Lachlan slept well overnight and his sleeping has improved a great deal overall since he was a toddler. These days there is usually one night a week where he wakes in the early hours of the morning for some reason. When Lachlan was younger this was a more frequent occurrence, often a few nights in a week.

Lachlan seemed more tired than usual this morning and Itsal searched for a break in Lachlan's clothing in order to nudge him in that spot to wake him up. Itsal jumped on and off the bed while Lachlan hid underneath his pillow. Both Lachlan and Itsal enjoy this game each weekday morning. After a while Lachlan sat up and Itsal sat on his pillow so that Lachlan was unable to lie back down. Lachlan did not become annoyed he just decided to get out of bed.

When Lachlan came into the lounge room he pointed up and down at the DVD piles, referring to their height which reminded me that I had moved part of the pile the night before as it had been blocking the television screen, and I had forgot to put them back. Lachlan indicated that I should put them back the way they were.

We are always amazed at how Lachlan communicates non-verbally precisely what he wants to say. He clearly indicated he'd noticed the change in height of the DVD towers.

This evening Lachlan requested to be tickled over and over again. He did this by gesturing him-tickling-himself while vocalising. When it was time for bed Lachlan asked for Itsal to join him. He pointed to the bed and then at Itsal and I gave Itsal the command to jump onto the bed. Itsal laid on Lachlan's feet and legs which gave him the pressure that he required and Lachlan fell asleep within a few minutes.

Chapter 5
May 2015

Friday 01/05/15

The morning routine went well but today the school bus came a little early and Lachlan was not quite ready as he still needed to put his shoes on. When I told him that the bus had arrived and that he needed to quickly put his shoes on, he did as he was asked. In the past it would have been a problem to rush or change any part of his routine, but not anymore.

Lachlan took his new drinks to school today and drank almost all of them. What a relief! He did drink a little less than usual, but I think he will get used to them. I am also encouraging him to drink only water in the evenings after brushing his teeth, which he did.

Saturday 02/05/15

Lachlan went to a new shopping centre without Itsal today as Debbie came to give Itsal a bath, so Itsal needed to stay home with me. While inside the shopping centre Lachlan looked at a large map of the shopping centre and chose three shops from it which he wanted to visit. After looking at the map, he was asked which way would be the correct way to go and he pointed up or down and to the names of the shops he wanted to visit. He knew exactly where he wanted to go. He looked at various toys, books, DVDs and CDs. Lachlan also rode on a children's ride which would not have happened before Itsal came along.

Even when Itsal and Lachlan are not together Lachlan has so much more confidence when he takes on new activities. Having Itsal has changed Lachlan a lot more than we ever thought possible. I do not know how Itsal has managed this, but he has. Lachlan enjoys walking with Itsal wherever they go and Lachlan is under the impression that he is also helping and guiding Itsal. He holds onto Itsal's harness because he does not want Itsal to get lost. When Lachlan is out with his family he prefers everyone in the group to stay together.

While training at Righteous Pups Australia Lachlan needed to challenge his parents being separated at the shopping centre as each parent needed to be assessed for competent handling of Itsal. After we arrived one parent would take Lachlan and Itsal and meet with the assessor, and strangely enough, because Itsal was there Lachlan did not seem to mind that one parent had disappeared into another part of the plaza. This alone was wonderful and new for us. While Chris had his handler assessment with Lachlan and Itsal, I had lunch at a restaurant with some of the other people from families we met at training and felt very delighted that this had now become a possibility.

While at home today, Itsal started to bark which is rare as he does not bark without a reason. Even though I had not heard anyone at the front door, I went to open it and investigate the reason for Itsal's barking. When I opened the door I found nobody there as I had expected, but Itsal still looked very concerned and the hairs on his back stood up. Something must have been wrong and I thought there may have been a stranger near the house that I was unaware of. While the door was open, Itsal pushed in front of me as if to protect me and looked down the driveway. Next he seized my wrist in his mouth and led me away from the door and into the kitchen which made it obvious he did not want me to go outside. Straight after, I heard a car which sped off loudly and furiously away from the street and I wondered whether there had been an altercation of some kind at that house.

As Lachlan was busy playing and did not try to go outside Itsal did not need to warn him. Itsal is aware of my role as Lachlan's mother and knows the things I am concerned about and he knows the right person to alert for the situation. Amazing isn't it!

There are times when Itsal overrides my wishes in order to carry out a request by Lachlan such as when Lachlan gestured and pointed for Itsal to join him in jumping on my bed. Itsal jumped onto my bed even though he had never been on it before, and knew he wasn't allowed on it. He looked at me and jumped off again. Itsal understood Lachlan's non-verbal request and I was pleased he did.

This evening Lachlan's respite carer and friend Pamela came over to care for Lachlan as there was a birthday party on tonight which adults in the family were going to. Lachlan was invited but we knew he would have been happier at home with Pamela, away from the noise and crowd of the birthday party. Lachlan had never spent an evening with Pamela before even though he has known her for five years and has spent many hours with her during the daytime. Lachlan looked a little confused when Pamela arrived at 6.00 p.m., but seemed happy. The evening went very well and Lachlan had a nice evening with Pamela and Itsal.

Pamela had completed the training to be one of Itsal's handlers which was a smaller version of the two-week training we ourselves did in Bendigo. Thanks for your support and dedication Pamela!

I remember how excited we all were to go to the Righteous Pups Australia training in Bendigo. Here Lachlan would meet his Autism Assistance dog and we could not wait! We also were to be trained in dog handling. We wondered what colour Lachlan's dog would be and whether it was a male or female. We could not wait to bring our dog home to live with us, but most of all we were excited about the assistance it would provide to Lachlan and the freedom we hoped it would give him from the many things he found overwhelming- noise, crowds, new places and situations and unexpected changes to his routine.

Once I remember we stopped on the way to an outing at a shopping centre to buy some lunch and the only the thing I remember about that day was Lachlan's reaction once we entered the shopping centre. He clung to me trying to keep me from moving further into the shopping centre and I decided that Lachlan and I would stay right where we were and Dad would go in and buy the lunch which wasn't going to take very long.

Lachlan stood still while he clung to me but became more distressed and started to cry and scream. I thought that perhaps if he sat inside a shopping trolley it may have helped so I tried to move towards the supermarket to get one while Lachlan clung to me crying and screaming. Eventually we reached the trolley and when Lachlan sat inside he became calmer as it created a buffer within its sides from everything else in the shopping centre.

The element of surprise is not one he appreciated at all. He liked to know exactly when, where, and with whom something would occur, and when an unexpected change took place he would become very distressed. Preparing Lachlan in advance for an outing with visuals and or iPad communication helped to some degree but nothing seemed to help when faced with an unexpected change to the routine.

Before Itsal came along there were still so many things Lachlan preferred to avoid even when he knew in advance what to expect. While Lachlan had tolerated shopping centres previously as a toddler, as he got older he could no longer, even though he would have been interested in some of the items in the shops.

As Lachlan needed to avoid so many places and situations, we felt his quality of life was affected in a huge way. He was missing out on life's enjoyment and learning experiences that other children took for granted. At the time we wondered if this would or could ever change as it seemed we had already tried everything. Even if the Righteous Pup made a small positive change for Lachlan we would have been happy.

Sunday 03/05/15

Itsal woke me at 6.00 a.m. At first I wondered if he thought it was a weekday and I should have been awake, or whether he just needed to use the toilet. A minute or two later I heard Lachlan had woken in his room and I knew this was the reason Itsal had woken me.

Today we needed to go shopping to buy another mini-trampoline as I noticed some of the straps had broken on the current one and, as well unsafe, it was probably not much fun to use either.

The mini-trampoline lives in the lounge room as it needs to be in a place where Lachlan can use it anytime he needs to. He uses it a lot as he has huge amounts of energy and needs to use up this energy as much as possible.

Lachlan also has a huge trampoline in the backyard which he uses every night unless it is raining. Lachlan enjoys jumping as it is natural way for him to use up his surplus energy.

Not using up his energy means that he will find it hard to get to sleep and we have found that he is more likely to awaken during the night if he has not had enough physical activity during the day. Swimming also uses up lots of his energy, which he also delights in.

We also needed to buy a new DVD player today as we noticed the screen on the current one had cracked. Most of the DVD players he has owned seem to last only a few months. He has had many DVD players before, as well as trampolines both large and small. These are some of his favourite things.

Tuesday 05/05/15

Lachlan woke up at 3.30 a.m. in a happy mood. We do not know why but 3.30 a.m. seems to be a common time for him to awaken. Sometimes he does not go back to sleep and if he does, it is usually after three hours. This time it was two hours, at 5.30 a.m. he fell asleep again.

Even though he must have been tired at school today, Lachlan's teacher reported that he had a great day.

Today I had an appointment with Lachlan's speech therapist Debbie regarding food issues. The last appointment had been two months ago and Debbie was impressed when I told her of all the positive changes which had taken place since we last spoke.

Lachlan now eats two different types of chips, biscuits, and a different type of juice, water, cheese sticks, and different types of bread. He has even tried Coca Cola a few times but did not really like it. Previously Lachlan would eat just one type of bread roll, one other type of loaf-bread, an occasional biscuit and the oat mixture mentioned earlier. The homework we need to do is to try some foods suggested by Debbie which are similar to the ones he already eats. First of all we need to leave them around so that he becomes used to the sight of the new food, then he needs to see other people eating it, and over time he might be willing to try it once he is used to the look and feel of it, probably after two or three months or more. With some foods it works, while for others it does not and we need to persevere over a number of months for any changes to occur.

After school today Lachlan went to the park and enjoyed the swings. In the past he would become upset when other children in the park sat on the swing the wrong way around or did something unusual such as stand on a swing. He does not become upset about this anymore. When Lachlan was much younger he would become upset if he even saw other children at the park and he would not get out of the car. If he was playing in the park and another child came along, he would scream. He is a very different boy at almost nine years of age and he really likes playing with other children now.

This evening Samantha came to visit on her way home. She had kindly picked up some of Lachlan's school shirts from the tailor where I had left them to have a panel sewn into the front of them as Lachlan had developed a habit of chewing them which caused them to tear.

When Samantha left Lachlan and I went outside to wave goodbye. Lachlan pointed to some airplane lights visible in the dark, and then pointed to a star and vocalised as he wanted me to also see it. When Samantha drove away, I asked him to say, "Bye to Samantha" and he said the word "Bye" for the first time ever. How exciting! I could not wait to tell Samantha.

Tonight Lachlan entertained himself as he danced around to The Wiggles songs while he drank one quarter of a bottle of water for the first time, which was fantastic as he usually only drinks juice.

Lachlan has never drunk milk except for breast milk. Lachlan was breastfed until age three-and-a-half when I suddenly needed to stop breastfeeding due to some medication I had to take. This was just as well as I was never quite sure how and when I would end the breastfeeding. Lachlan was very attached to breastfeeding and saw no problem with having it any place or any time he liked. As he was getting older and much bigger, I tried to reduce the amount of feeds hoping he would grow out of wanting it. Being a reserved person, I did not really feel comfortable with breastfeeding him as a toddler in public. Lachlan was eating quite well at this stage and I felt he did not really need the breast milk as much, particularly on an outing. Well, he didn't see it the same way.

As Lachlan started to get bigger he would climb onto my lap and lay down. At first, I did not realise that this meant he wanted breastmilk, so I asked him "What are you trying to do?" and before long he started to call breast milk "Do" maybe because it was an easy word to say or because that was the word he heard when he wanted breastmilk. Calling it "Do" was actually very good, as when we were out in public and he started screaming out for "Do" no one else knew what he was talking about. It would have been much worse if he had shouted out more obvious words, "Breastmilk" or something else!

139

Whenever Lachlan would see an unclothed mannequin in a shop he would point at it and shout "Do". Sometimes when he saw bras in a shop he would shout out "Do". It seemed that seeing either the bras or unclothed mannequins reminded him of breastmilk, at which point he would want to have it straight away, right there and then. He would point to my breasts and say "Do" and start saying it louder and louder until he screamed it out. How was I going to get out of this? Time to go home, I thought.

Lachlan had previously learned to use PECS (a picture exchange communication system while at early intervention and speech therapy) so that he could request his needs. Using this system, Lachlan chose the picture which he thought best represented breastmilk which was the picture for "Happy" which made me wonder if breastmilk really made him this happy, or did he think my breast looked like the picture? When the time came that he needed to stop breastfeeding he was quite happy to go along with my request and just had a cuddle on my lap instead while we read a story. Stopping "Do" worked out so much easier than I had thought.

I really thought at this stage there wasn't much milk left and breastfeeding had become more of a habit which Lachlan found comforting. He was happy to have the same amount of attention without the breastmilk which worked out very well for both of us. I thought Lachlan was very clever to have discovered two ways of communicating that he wanted breastmilk.

He was clever enough to choose one of the few words he was able to say as well as finding a picture to represent it.

Lachlan was quite tired this evening and fell asleep by 9.00 p.m. which was unusual for him, and good for all. What a fantastic day Lachlan had.

Wednesday 06/05/15

This evening Samantha and her friend John came for dinner. Throughout the evening Lachlan watched various YouTube videos in different languages, as he often does. If he is watching Mickey Mouse in another language which we do not understand, we usually assume the English equivalent is what he is hearing. Well, not this time. John speaks Spanish and when he heard the Spanish version of Mickey Mouse playing he listened to it carefully. On hearing it from another room, John looked shocked and went in with Lachlan to investigate. He came back to tell us that the voiceover on the Spanish Mickey Mouse video should not be heard by children as it contained crude words and swearing. We would not have known, so I was pleased that John had told us.

Later on during the evening, John spoke to Lachlan and told him in Spanish that it is was almost bed time. Lachlan became slightly upset on hearing this, but then we knew that he understood the Spanish words. John was pleasantly surprised that Lachlan also understood these Spanish words. This is another of Lachlan's talents.

Saturday 09/05/14

This morning we went to the bakery to buy Lachlan's usual bread rolls. Hong and her husband who run the bakery, bake and keep Lachlan's favourite bread rolls for him each day. Lachlan is very fond of Hong and she always encourages Lachlan to participate in the activity of buying the rolls. She encourages him to hand her the money and she hands the bread rolls and change to him, and she watches as Lachlan puts the change in his pocket. I do not know where the change ends up, perhaps under the car seat, but I never see it again.

Today in the bakery, Hong had a beige coloured bantam chicken walking around the shop. Knowing that Lachlan's birthday was coming up soon, Hong offered it to for him as a birthday present. Lachlan loves chickens and Hong seemed to know that about him and I assumed I had told her in a previous conversation.

We would have liked to have accepted it and taken it home but thought it may not work out with our cat Boogle, who is a Birman Himalayan. She is brown and fluffy with a black face. Boogle really does not like other animals at all as she is very scared of them. Even a bird singing in a nearby tree frightens her. Itsal is the only animal she is not frightened of as he avoids her and is very cautious as she hisses at him occasionally. We really could not take the chicken home.

In two days it will be Lachlan's 9th birthday, and tomorrow we are taking Lachlan and his cousin Steven on a steam train ride. We think that Lachlan would prefer the train ride instead of a birthday party. Steven will be having a sleepover with Lachlan at home and we will head off in the morning for the train ride.

Lachlan was awake during the night which is not unusual for him. This has always happened since Lachlan was a baby and he has not been disturbed by it. He is always in a happy mood despite being awake for two or three hours at times.

Sunday 10/05/15

Lachlan and Steven had fun during the afternoon, jumping on the trampoline and showing each other computer games.

Steven slept in a separate room to Lachlan. The next morning he commented that Lachlan had been awake for a long time in the middle of the night. Steven seemed really surprised about this and he was even more surprised when I answered, "Was he?" Itsal would not allow anything to go wrong and I know he would have woken us if needed. Being sure that I would wake up if I had sensed Lachlan was disturbed, either by hearing or sensing it, I was able to sleep even though Lachlan had woken.

We all headed out for the steam train ride, Itsal included. Lachlan was so excited when he saw the steam train, and the boys each picked their seats near the window. They hardly spoke as they observed the country scenery from their windows. Itsal seemed quite happy and comfortable on the train. When we did the training at Righteous Pups Australia, we went on a similar steam train ride which the children all loved, so I knew Itsal was used to trains.

When the train arrived back at the station, Lachlan and Steven looked around the train museum. They climbed on and off numerous different trains. Lachlan had a fantastic day with his family and Itsal seemed to enjoy it as well.

Monday 11/05/15

Lachlan's 9th Birthday.

Today we went shopping but didn't take Itsal with us. He had such a busy day yesterday and seemed very tired and I was interested to see how Lachlan would find the shopping centre without him.

When Lachlan awoke he was not as happy as usual perhaps because he had another night where he stayed awake for two hours. I hoped that the shopping would cheer him up. After being shown his PECS folder Lachlan requested to buy a DVD and this made him excited.

At the shops Lachlan headed straight to the DVD section and instead of choosing one DVD he chose three. I think he realised that on his birthday, I would probably not have said no. Next he was ready to go home and watch the new DVDs, but first I told him we needed to buy a few groceries.

When Itsal is with us Lachlan seems to think a lot less about his environment which he often finds totally overstimulating due to the crowd and noise level. Lachlan was unhappy to do grocery shopping and needed encouragement; this isn't necessary when Itsal is with us as Lachlan is more settled and happy to follow Itsal while holding onto his harness.

Once inside the grocery shop, I asked Lachlan to hold onto the handle of the trolley as I could not be sure

147

he would have followed me. Most of the time Lachlan held onto the trolley as we walked around the shop. At times he would let go of the trolley and when I asked him to hold onto it again he did so, which helped him to stay focused on the task. For many years Lachlan sat inside the shopping trolley until he became too big and it became unsafe. Lachlan can now walk independently holding Itsal's harness.

Once at the checkout Lachlan helped load the groceries onto the counter. He was happy to lift heavier items and any items which were not green such as broccoli.

This afternoon we waited for Samantha to arrive, after which we lit the candles on Lachlan's pink birthday cake that he chose for himself. He also chose a car decoration for the top of the cake. He did not eat any of the cake but was equally as pleased to see others eating it.

Friday 15/05/15

This morning when we did Lachlan's morning wake up routine, I could not believe that Itsal pressed the start button on the DVD player which started Lachlan's favourite DVD. Lachlan watched the DVD for a short time in bed before he got dressed for school. Itsal had not been asked to interact with the DVD player and I would not have known he was able to do this. Itsal also knew the exact time to do it. He is incredible!

Lachlan has had an excellent week. His teacher reported that he had done some great work on the computer at school and with reading.

This evening just as I was about to begin Lachlan's teeth brushing routine, he grabbed the toothbrush from my hand. I asked him to brush his teeth and held onto his hand with mine over his to support the movements while counting to one hundred. I slowly removed my hand which meant Lachlan was brushing his teeth independently for the first time!

Saturday 16/05/15

Today was Lachlan's first soccer game for the season as the last two previously scheduled games were cancelled due to wet weather. Lachlan seemed very pleased to be back after a long break. Lachlan stayed for half the game then wanted to leave. Sometimes it takes a little while for him to get back into the routine again. This is Lachlan's third soccer season and he has come a long way since he first started.

At first Lachlan was reluctant to get out of the car when he saw so many other people on the oval. I remember one of the other parents telling me that their son had stayed in the toilet block on the oval during the game, perhaps for the same reason as Lachlan, and eventually had become used to the idea and now enjoys soccer. Lachlan is proud of the two trophies he won for the last two seasons.

Lachlan went to the park after soccer. When he left he pointed in the direction he wanted the car to follow which led us to another park. He remembered the way to each park and directed us to four in total. One of the parks he had only been to once before which was a very long time ago. After lots of playing in parks he came home very tired.

Lachlan never forgets a route and school bus drivers have often said that if they take a wrong turn or different route Lachlan will point out their mistake. He does not need electronic navigation.

During the evening Lachlan typed the words "Mickey Mouse Francois" into the computer and found a French episode of Mickey Mouse which he watched on YouTube. I hoped that it would not contain French swear words like the Spanish one which he had found previously.

Sunday 17/05/15

We went to church this morning and as usual Lachlan wanted to play outside. If we arrive during the singing, Lachlan is usually happy to stay inside at the church service as he likes the music. Today he chose to go outside straight away. It is his choice.

Today we did not see our friend Karen at church. Lachlan is always very excited to see Karen as she pays him special attention and communicates with signs which Lachlan understands and likes.

It is not absolutely necessary to communicate with signs for Lachlan as he understands words and uses pictures (PECS) as well as iPad communication. We think it beneficial for Lachlan to have as many ways as possible to communicate. It is very handy to know the 'toilet' sign, as well as 'more' and 'finished' signs. Those three seem to be the most important.

Quite often, we arrive late for church and we cannot sneak in without anyone noticing, as Lachlan vocalises and he is very excited to be there. The church we attend is a place where Lachlan and his family can go and we know that he is truly accepted there. Almost everyone knows him and there is a big photo of him and Itsal in the foyer of the church. Everyone at church is always happy to see Lachlan, and Itsal is very popular, of course. Sometimes Karen invites Lachlan to play outside with her which allows us to attend the church service inside. How very thoughtful, and Lachlan likes it as well. Thank you, Karen and Guy, for your support.

As Lachlan had been promised a trip to the shops this afternoon we did not stay for morning tea at church today. At the shops Lachlan choose a giant bread stick and ate it all and enjoyed window shopping and riding on some children's rides.

Tuesday 19/05/15

This morning Itsal started barking near the door to alert us of a stranger outside. When I opened the door he stood in front of me, not allowing me to go out unless he went first. I could not see any strangers nearby but I heard workmen had arrived at the building site next door and they had come closer to the house than Itsal liked. Itsal went and sat on Lachlan's feet which prevented him from moving in case of a threat outside. After taking another look outside, I let Itsal know there was nothing to worry about, so he relaxed on his mat and our morning routine continued.

Itsal knows he'll be paid no attention while Lachlan's school day routine is in operation. When I fed Itsal this morning, he sat and looked at me and did not want to eat his food. I wondered if I had done something wrong, or whether he was perhaps unwell. He continued to sit near the food while looking at me. I did not know what was going on, but assumed he would eat his food later on when he was ready.

After this, I fed our cat Boogle and when I came back inside Itsal looked at me and then started eating his food. I then realised that Itsal's reluctance was due to him being fed before Boogle as she is usually fed first before Itsal. Itsal knew this was not part out of the usual routine. Sorry for any inconvenience caused, Itsal.

Lachlan had a lovely day at school and was happy to be home as usual. He had his usual afternoon tea, a chocolate chip muffin while he played with his DVD player and then headed off to the park to play.

This evening Lachlan read his school book as part of his homework. I noticed that these books were also written in Braille. I wonder if he would be able to learn Braille the way he has learned different languages. He had not yet shown an interest in it.

Thursday 21/05/15

Lachlan has had another great week, so far. He slept well overnight and was very happy to wake up and get ready for school. But today, the alarm did not work so when I woke up there was around ten to fifteen minutes for Lachlan to prepare for school before the bus arrived!

After taking Lachlan his DVD player, I told him that he needed to get up straight away today as we were running late. He seemed to understand this and complied with getting dressed swiftly even though he usually likes to watch DVDs and take his time with the morning routine. This wouldn't have been possible when Lachlan was younger as he was unable to skip any parts of his usual routines. He would have been extremely stressed and probably had a meltdown. These days he copes with unexpected changes although I get the feeling he does prefer to have a stable routine so that he knows what to expect next.

This afternoon Lachlan came home from school without his shoes and no one at school seemed to know what had happened to them. I asked Lachlan about them and he laughed. We may never know what happened to them. Maybe they would show up somewhere at school eventually.

This evening Lachlan played some music in his room and danced around. When the time came, I reminded him he could play two more songs and then it was time for bed. He replayed the same song over and over and I wondered if he thought it counted as one song. I think this may have been a delaying tactic so next he was told the current song was being played for the last time before bed. He was happy enough with that.

Saturday 23/05/15

Today Lachlan went to soccer with Dad. It seemed to work out better to park a few streets away and walk to the soccer field as it gave Lachlan extra time to get used to the idea of being on a field full of people as he can find it overwhelming at times. Today, Lachlan waited in the queues for his turn on the activities which included jumping in and out of ladders on the ground, moving the ball around with his foot and kicking it into the nets. He kicked the soccer ball long distances many times and easily, as his legs are incredibly strong. As this was the second week back, it seemed as though Lachlan was getting used to soccer again, as last week he wanted to leave early.

This afternoon Samantha and John came to visit and I noticed that Lachlan had put on the Spanish version of Mickey Mouse, to make John feel at home perhaps.

While the rest of us chatted outside, Lachlan went and got his small purple bike that he rides occasionally. The purple bike is low to the ground and Lachlan rides it by pushing it along with his feet. He also likes to ride it very fast down the sloping driveway which is frightening to watch as we have to stop him from riding past the driveway and onto the road. He pointed to the horn and said "Go" which jogged my memory that he had bought a new police alarm horn for his bike a week ago and now wanted it to be fitted to his bike.

Lachlan handed it to Samantha and John and they kindly attached it to Lachlan's other bike. He was so excited when he pressed the button and a deafening loud siren was heard. We all covered our ears while Lachlan jumped up and down excitedly and then pressed it again. He was having a fantastic time! I thought it would be interesting taking the bike to the park with the loud siren.

This evening Lachlan was very tired as he had woken up at 5.30 a.m. this morning. He was too tired to play for very long in his room but enjoyed watching his water lamp with electronic jellyfish swimming inside it. When it was time to switch it off, he waved to the jellyfish.

Sunday 24/05/15

This morning Lachlan watched cartoons in German and Malaysian languages. I had made toast with jam for breakfast with different types of breads and one crust. Lachlan's speech therapist Debbie had told us it was good idea to mix up different types of bread making them look slightly different to each other. This would make it less likely Lachlan would become tired of eating that same food.

Lachlan inspected the different looking pieces of toast, turning them upside down and touching the other side of each piece. To him, these were not slightly different, they were very different. I pretended not to notice as he inspected several pieces of toast before he ate any. This time he even ate the crust which was very good, excellent!

Lachlan went into Sydney today and had his first ride on a tram, which he loved. He looked in his favourite toy shop which had many different types of trains before he went to the park and had a good run around.

During the bath-time routine I noticed that Lachlan had become much better at brushing his teeth. Next we did flossing which he did not mind and as there is an upcoming dental appointment, we prepared for it by practicing an examination with a pretend dentist's mirror. This has helped Lachlan prepare for dental appointments in the past.

We took turns with the mirror and when it was my turn I hoped that Lachlan would not push the mirror too far into my throat as he had done once before. I was a little guarded!

Monday 25/05/15

Lachlan was awake from 4.00 a.m. to 5.30 a.m. this morning, which is not unusual. When it was time to wake up and prepare for school, Lachlan was so tired that the noise coming from the DVD player did not wake him like it usually would. Itsal was also tired today, so the two of them continued to sleep as the DVD played loudly and the light shone into the room through the curtains I had opened.

Ten minutes later I tried again to wake Lachlan up, and this time I needed Itsal's help. After I gave Itsal a command he jumped off Lachlan's bed. Itsal found a gap in Lachlan's pyjamas which exposed part of his back and nudged him there to wake him up. It worked and Lachlan turned around and started to watch his DVD. Next Itsal nudged the DVD player as if to remind me that I needed to take it out of the room. Lachlan usually follows the DVD player and now he would follow and get dressed for school. Which he did.

The school bus was late today. As Lachlan waited he enjoyed watching DVDs for longer than usual. It was very cold today so I tried to persuade Lachlan to wear his woollen school jacket but he pushed it away and signed "Finished" making it very clear he did not want to wear it, thank you. He was quite pleased when the bus came even though he had just selected a DVD to watch and now had to put it down.

Tuesday 26/05/15

This morning Lachlan awoke at 3.00 a.m. It was very cold in his room so I put his heater on and covered him with an extra blanket. Thirty minutes later he became drowsy and eventually fell asleep after he had held my hand for fifty minutes, which was faster than usual. I was unsure why he had fallen back to sleep so easily this time and hoped it would become a new pattern.

When it came time for Lachlan to wake up and prepare for school he did not seem tired as he was just fifty minutes short of a good night's sleep. He did not want to wear his woollen jacket again, even though it was very cold outside. Lachlan is not sensitive to cold weather and I think he would prefer to feel cold rather than risk becoming overheated by wearing the jacket.

Wednesday 27/05/15

Lachlan's school day went smoothly and when he came home his school shoes which had disappeared at school a few days ago, had returned in his bag.

After school Lachlan was in a very happy mood and wanted me to sit beside him while he played on the computer. He kept his arm around my neck (some might call it a bear hug) while he ate a bread roll and I could feel bread crumbs dropping into my hair! Funny!

Lachlan asked me to type various words into the toolbar and when I made a mistake, he decided to do his own typing. He typed 'Little red' into the computer and 'Little Red Riding Hood' came up. He did not choose any of those words and I wondered if he may have been looking for 'Little Robots' so I typed it into the computer. Lachlan deleted the words I had typed and typed in 'Little Red Tractor' instead. He found what he had been looking for and now he was happy. I stood up when Lachlan released me from his bear hug and he said "Mum" as he gestured for me to stay longer. He has said

"Mum" occasionally before and it is always extremely wonderful whenever he speaks.

While I was busy typing on the computer two people came to the front door. I intended to answer it but needed to finish typing the sentence I was working on. Before I was able to finish the sentence, I heard the people at the door having an argument about something which caused Itsal to run to the door and start growling at them. When they heard his growls they left swiftly and did not knock on our door.

This afternoon Itsal sat next to me for two hours while I read a book. Afterwards I wondered if he needed to go outside to the toilet as I remembered he had been inside the entire day. Unlike other dogs I've had, Itsal does not become desperate about the toilet – he waits instead for someone to go to the back-door area to let him out into the backyard. Occasionally he will sit next to the back door and wait until someone opens it. Most of the time he seems to wait until someone else thinks about it first. Itsal has manners.

There has only been one occasion when Itsal really could not wait to go to the toilet. It was when I was being assessed as a dog handler for public access certification at Righteous Pups Australia in Bendigo. Now that I had completed the two-week training course I was ready for the assessment which would be held in one of the local shopping centres in Bendigo.

On the morning of the assessment it had been a rush to make sure we arrived at the shopping centre at the set appointment time. We made it in time for the assessment and we were not late to meet Jenny from Righteous Pups. We met Jenny at the shopping centre entrance and Lachlan, Itsal and I made our way to the shop where we had agreed to meet for the assessment.

Lachlan was a little stressed inside the shop as he wanted to do his own thing and go shopping instead of waiting while the assessment took place. Jen asked some of the questions required of the assessment and also spoke to a girl and her mother inside the shop and asked whether they would assist with the assessment by patting Itsal. The girl seemed excited and her mother was very happy for her daughter to help out by patting Itsal during the assessment so that his reaction could be gauged. When the girl patted Itsal he did as he was supposed to, and barely made any reaction. Until now we were all doing very well.

We walked outside the store headed towards the exit with Jenny when we stopped and talked about the assessment. Jenny told me there was just one more task left to complete for the assessment and while we spoke about it, I noticed Itsal had stopped and stood still. Jenny noticed that Itsal had begun to urinate and there was nothing we could do except wait until he was finished.

Just then I remembered during the morning rush that poor Itsal had not been given an extra opportunity to go to the toilet. Oh no! Jenny was very understanding and asked me if I had my clean-up kit (which dog handlers should carry at all times), to clean up the urine. I realised I had left the clean-up kit behind at the house in the morning rush as I thought mainly of Lachlan at the time to make sure he was prepared for the day.

I looked into my handbag and found a small packet of tissues which was the only option I had to offer to clean up the huge puddle poor Itsal had left. Jenny kindly replied, "You have only had small dogs before, haven't you?" Jenny advised a security worker in the shopping mall of the hazard and set about cleaning Itsal's puddle with the clean-up kit she had in her back pack. Thanks for your understanding Jenny!

Friday 29/05/15

Today Lachlan and his class went on a school excursion for Indigenous National Reconciliation Week. Inside the hall Lachlan and his class performed the song "We are Australian". The school sent a photo which showed Lachlan on stage and some of the children singing. When Lachlan came home and I asked about it, he seemed very pleased and proud.

While Lachlan was at school I shopped for some shoes for him. I had drawn an outline around his foot on a piece of paper so that I would be able to buy shoes which were the right size. This was much easier than taking Lachlan to buy the shoes as he is really not interested in shopping for shoes or clothes; however

DVDs are a different matter. It is easier for both of us to do the shoe shopping this way.

The new shoes I bought were the same style as ones he already has, just a different colour. In the past I have bought many pairs of shoes which Lachlan would not wear for some reason. There had been boots, running shoes and slippers which he had rejected. Once I bought a pair of running shoes which had flashing lights on them. I was sure he would like them but Lachlan was horrified when he saw them and would not allow them in his wardrobe at all. Lachlan prefers plain shoes which are very comfortable and then he is happy to wear them.

When Lachlan came home from school I showed him the new black shoes and he wanted to try them on. He tried one of the shoes on and wanted to take it off straight away. He was not ready to wear them yet, so I left them in the lounge room where he could see them so that he would become accustomed to them.

When Lachlan first started school, I remember leaving the new school shoes out for a week prior to school starting. He would wear them for a few minutes each day until he got used to them.

Lachlan has come a long way since then and he now likes new shoes and clothes. When I asked him which of the four new shirts he liked best he picked a grey one with a skateboard on it. The other ones were green, white and blue. It seems that he likes dark, plain coloured clothes.

This evening after dinner Lachlan watched an episode of Mickey Mouse (in a language of which I was unsure) as well as an episode of The Wiggles in a foreign language. Next Lachlan sought out and used his iPad to request a snack. He selected the buttons so that it spoke out "I want toast with jam". This is excellent!

When unpacking Lachlan's school bag this afternoon, I found a school award that Lachlan had received for typing his weekend news out on the computer. Well done Lachlan!

Saturday 30/05/15

Lachlan awoke at 6.00 a.m. He went to soccer where he was greeted by some of the other players which he seemed pleased about. During the game he kicked some very good goals. He also participated in an activity where the players stood in a square and each person kicked their ball from the top of a cone to the middle of the square, then retrieved the ball.

Itsal stayed home with me today as Debbie (his groomer) was due to give him a bath again. When she arrived he happily went with her to the mobile van waiting outside. He is used to the bathing routine. When he came back inside he sat and looked at me to let me know he wanted something. What was it, I wondered? I opened the door to let him outside in case he wanted the toilet but when he came back inside he just sat and looked at me again. It was not the toilet he wanted. When I asked him what he wanted he looked at the spot where his bed is usually placed and I realised that is what he wanted - I had not yet put his bed in its right place, and when I did Itsal climbed onto it and went to sleep.

Meanwhile Lachlan went to three different parks to play for the afternoon. He liked the swing at one of the parks and at another he liked walking on the wall there. He wanted to ride a merry-go-round at another park. Once he has visited a park he always remembers everything in it especially rides which he is fond of. At some parks there are particular swings he likes or walking tracks, rides or walls.

Lachlan also knows how to get to each place as he has a phenomenal memory and can give directions by pointing. If you follow his lead he will take you all around Sydney to his favourite parks and places. He also remembers where supermarkets are even when we haven't been to them before.

Lachlan once led us to a newly built supermarket which was off a main road. We do not know how he knew it was there. He marched in and went straight to his favourite section (the bakery section) and picked out a giant bread stick. It always looks so funny, a child eating a whole giant bread stick in public, but he prefers this to fast food or junk food.

Chapter 6
June 2015

Monday 01/06/15

Lachlan had a dental appointment booked for today. We have been practicing each night with the pretend dentist mirror and Lachlan will now allow a quick examination with me holding the mirror pretending to be a dentist. He will need to have some work done under general anaesthetic and I am grateful that this can happen during the next school holidays so that Lachlan will not need to take any time off school. The plan is to buy a mask from the pharmacy and practice with it each day so that when the time comes for him to be anaesthetised he will be familiar with using a mask. Hopefully this will help him feel more comfortable.

After the dental appointment we went to a nearby shopping centre. The shopping centre was known to Lachlan and he also knew which shops he wanted to visit as soon as he arrived. He looked in various shops for DVDs but it seemed that he was looking for something in particular which he could not find, so we went from shop to shop while he searched. Lachlan remembered the layout of each shop and exactly where the DVDs were in each one. He also enjoyed looking at the children's rides, and rode on one of them, a carousel, as it spun around.

Lachlan sat in the food court and ate his usual lunch (which was bought from home as he does not eat fast food). He looked at the salad I was eating for lunch and signed "Finished" which meant that he did not like the look of it and wanted it to go away. Nowadays he can tolerate sitting at the same table even if he does not like the look of foods others are eating. He sat at the table while I ate the salad. The main thing that I noticed about this was that he was happy and not uncomfortable to sit there while I ate my lunch. Since having Itsal, Lachlan has been able do this at the shopping centre. Previously he found it far too overwhelming and would run off, if he agreed to enter the shopping centre at all.

Lachlan eventually found a DVD he wanted after he had looked in several shops, and then he was ready to go home. He came along to the supermarket while I bought some groceries and at the checkout Lachlan put the items onto the conveyer belt. It is always quite funny to watch him do this as he enjoys helping but wants to minimise the time he touches the items, especially vegetables! He swiftly tossed them onto the conveyer belt.

Overall, Lachlan is much less sensitive to touching vegetables than previously, but he still does not like green fruits or vegetables or fruits with unusual skin, such as kiwi fruit. Debbie's sessions have helped a lot with this as she has advised us on ways to expose Lachlan to different food types by seeing and interacting with them, and he has become less sensitive to them.

In the afternoon Danielle came to cut Lachlan's hair. Before she arrived I showed him three PECS pictures; Danielle, haircut and present, which he acknowledged as he nodded and touched his hair. I have noticed that after haircuts Lachlan is always touching his hair and seems to enjoy the new shortness of it.

Danielle did the haircut inside today as it was cold and dark outside. Lachlan mostly complied with the hair cutting, while we all chatted. Towards the end he wanted the haircut to finish so Danielle tried to finish it as quick as she could. As usual, Danielle did a fantastic job. Lachlan's hair looked great and Danielle gave Lachlan a gift which was a Mickey Mouse straw which her mum Linda had bought back from overseas. Lachlan liked the straw and played with it in the bath while he washed the loose hair away. Thank you Danielle-you are fantastic! You make life much easier for Lachlan.

Saturday 06/06/15

Lachlan played soccer today and won a medal. We were all so proud of him and he was proud of himself also. The other players congratulated him and he seemed very pleased with himself. After he arrived home, he wore the medal proudly for the rest of the day and looked at it every now and then.

This evening while doing the bedtime routine, Lachlan and I read a story. He seemed a little drowsy as he listened to the story and when it finished he became lively again and jumped around while he played in his room. As I was tired I lay on Lachlan's bed and told him that I would sleep there which made him laugh. Lachlan put his face next to mine and I told him I was going to sleep now and he laughed again. He looked at me directly in the eye and I said, "Good looking" which I thought might encourage him to make more eye contact in the future. I have noticed that when he has felt amused or interested in a subject he has made more eye contact. I asked him "What colour are my eyes?" and he signed "Green". When I asked him the same question about his eyes he signed "Blue".

Lachlan looked at my face for much longer than usual while I talked about eye colour and I wondered how I could encourage the same in the future to assist with his social skills. Lachlan obviously had noticed that people had different eye colours. Lachlan loves colourful things so perhaps that was why he seemed so interested.

When Lachlan was a toddler one of his therapists suggested using stickers to attract his attention which I would place between my eyes. When Lachlan noticed the small star sticker on my face he would remove it and put it between his eyes and go back to playing whatever was entertaining him at the time.

Tonight during the bedtime routine Lachlan tucked my hand underneath his chest, laid upon it, and fell asleep about forty minutes later. Just as I heard his breathing had changed (which meant he was asleep), Itsal started to growl. Oh no! Itsal was also asleep and must have been having a nightmare. Whispering, I told him to be quiet and he woke briefly and fell back to sleep. Thankfully, Lachlan was undisturbed!

Sunday 07/06/15

Today Lachlan went on an outing to the city. When he arrived he visited one of his favourite shopping centres at Broadway. He looked in various shops and the more unusual they were the more he liked them. He enjoyed browsing in small shops which sold mixed goods and he checked each aisle and corner of the shops he looked in.

Next he went to the railway station where he saw five double decker buses. He rode on a green and yellow bus and wanted to sit on the top floor. He was very surprised and excited when it started moving all of a sudden. The round trip lasted twenty minutes and Lachlan would have been quite happy to stay on the bus as he did not really want to get off until he noticed some steam coming from a parked steam train ready to depart at the station.

Lachlan quickly left the bus once he saw the steam train. First he looked at the engine and when asked about various parts on the outside of the train, he pointed to them as he remembered all the names of the parts.

Next he boarded the train which was full of passengers and was due to depart five minutes later. He looked in two of the carriages, one sold souvenirs which he was very interested in, and in the second carriage he sat for a moment as he tried out the seat. The train was about to depart, so we stepped off and watched it as it left the platform. Lachlan was very excited as he watched the steam train move off the platform.

Next he looked inside some antique single train carriages which were on display, and we walked back to the main concourse where Lachlan noticed a jazz band playing and marched over to have a closer look. His eyes locked on the tuba player as he walked closer and closer to examine the tuba. The tuba player noticed Lachlan's interest and started to move forward from the line-up. He bent down, so that Lachlan could touch the tuba. Lachlan was thrilled. The player played a lot of different notes to see Lachlan's reaction to them. Lachlan kept on touching the tuba and the player seemed very happy for that to happen.

Next to the band, they had constructed a mock-up of the front of a tram so that visitors could take a photo of themselves in the cab wearing the tram driver's hat. Lachlan looked briefly at the fake tram, and then ran back to the tuba player. He had another closer look at the fake tram before going to a nearby park. The park had a huge rope climbing frame and Lachlan climbed to the top, easily. He liked playing on the swings while he enjoyed the busyness of the main road with all the cars and noises coming from the traffic. On the ground in the park there were large geometric shapes of different colours which he walked on. Next he looked at the duck pond (ducks are some of his favourite animals), and then we went back to the shopping centre.

This evening, one of Lachlan's DVDs did not seem to be working. He gestured for me to put it on to the new television to watch, which we had bought just a few days before and had not used yet. I asked Lachlan to wait as I tried to figure out how the new remote control worked and which of the buttons operated the DVD player. As I pressed the different buttons on the remote control and television set to see what they did, I heard a banging noise outside. I went to investigate the noise but did not see anything unusual and Itsal was not concerned.

When I returned a few minutes later, I saw that Lachlan had worked the new television set out and was watching his DVD in German, one of his favourite languages. How could he have worked this out so fast?

Monday 08/06/15

While I was still half asleep this morning, I heard some noises in my bedroom. I could feel something next my bed but for some reason I felt too tired to open my eyes. As I am waking up I am realising that something unusual was happening in the room, somebody or something was in it. It was still dark and very early as my alarm had not sounded yet. Even though it was a public holiday today, I had set the alarm as I needed to complete some tasks before Lachlan woke up.

Although I was half asleep I knew it wasn't Lachlan in the room as he wouldn't have been so subtle. Still being half asleep, I thought that it must be Itsal in the room. Itsal, yes, that's what was going on. As I slowly started to wake due of the activity in the room, I wondered, still with my eyes closed if it was Itsal. Itsal or what else? A ghost perhaps? Now I really was hoping that it was Itsal, and I opened my eyes.

Itsal was sitting right next to my bed, near my face looking at me. He did not lick my face, thankfully. I could hear that Lachlan was awake, walking around the house and I knew this was the reason Itsal had woken me. He wanted me to know that Lachlan was up walking around unsupervised. It was 5.30 a.m. and Lachlan had just switched his light on and gone to fetch himself a DVD to watch.

Occasionally Lachlan came out of his room and signed "More" while he looked at his DVD collection which meant he wanted me to suggest a DVD for him to watch. I suggested some, but he shook his head in disagreement. Eventually I made a suitable suggestion which he was happy with and after I removed it from the collection he ran off into his room and watched it. He changed the DVD a few more times and signed "Help" to request access to the ones toward the bottom of the pile as he did not want them to fall, should they be disturbed.

While I was busy in the kitchen, I noticed that Lachlan had been in bed for some time and had not changed the DVD. When I looked into his room, I noticed that the DVD was still playing loudly and that Lachlan had fallen asleep. I tried to turn the volume down without waking him, but I was unable to as he held onto it, so I left him to sleep. He slept undisturbed by the loudness of the movie which played in the background.

Lachlan slept until 12.45 p.m. which is the latest he had ever slept in. I wondered if he was a little unwell as he did not want to go out (which was unusual), except to the bakery. He was quite happy to stay home and he played with his toys and watched DVDs. He coughed at times and I wondered whether he had caught a cold or flu.

Thursday 11/06/15

This morning Itsal woke me around 5.30 a.m. While I slowly woke up I heard him walking around in the background. He stood right next to me as he waited for me to wake up. He did not touch me as he knew that standing next to me would probably be enough to wake me. When I woke up I checked on Lachlan and I noticed that he had kicked his blankets off. I knew this was the reason Itsal has woken me as he knows that I often cover Lachlan with his blankets during the night. How incredible that Itsal is able to decide on things he should be concerned about!

Friday 12/06/15

This morning as Itsal woke me once again as he sat near my bed. As I wondered what the time was, my alarm sounded and Itsal nudged me and wagged his tail. It seemed as though he had been waiting for the alarm to sound. He nudged me again and I could tell by the way he acted with a sense of urgency, that he needed my attention immediately. He raced outside to the toilet when I opened the back door. Nice of him to wait until my alarm sounded before he woke me up!

As usual Itsal helped wake Lachlan to get ready for school. Most of the time Lachlan is happy to see Itsal. He jumped onto Lachlan's bed and Lachlan hid his face under his boomerang pillow which stopped Itsal coming too close to his face. As typical for the morning routine, Itsal looked for a gap in Lachlan's clothing and when he did not find one, he nudged Lachlan's foot with his snout. Lachlan pushed Itsal and he jumped off the bed. Itsal waited for a command before he got back onto the bed.

After another command Itsal got back onto Lachlan's bed then leapt off again. Lachlan wanted him back on the bed yet again so he pointed to the bed and said "Go". Itsal obeyed which prompted Lachlan to spring up and begin the day. Itsal wagged his tail and followed Lachlan to the bathroom where he dressed in his school uniform.

Saturday 13/06/15

Lachlan played soccer this morning and today the players had group and individual yearly photos taken. Lachlan happily posed for his photo.

This afternoon I found Lachlan looking inside my handbag. He had found my wallet and was looking through the many cards inside it. Finally, he found the one he was looking for which was my banking card. As I was wondering what he wanted with this, he went to his PECS folder and picked out the pictures; 'Go', 'Shop' and 'DVD'. Lachlan had picked the right card from the forty cards which were in my wallet.

Sunday 14/06/15

We went to church today and Lachlan sat in the church service for longer than he had ever done before. He sat and happily ate his bread rolls during the service while Itsal lay at his feet. The people at church are used to seeing Lachlan eat bread rolls during the service and nobody seems to mind. He enjoyed hearing the singing and instruments being played and sometimes after the service he will go up onto the stage to take a closer look at the instruments. Sometimes Jean plays a song on the piano for him and sings to him. Lachlan loves this as he enjoys her beautiful singing voice. Another time he was delighted to have been allowed a turn on the drum set.

Monday 15/06/15

Lachlan had a happy day at school, but of course was pleased to come home. For afternoon tea he ate three large cookies and then went to the library. At the library he chose three DVDs as well as some books and was excited to bring them home to watch.

Lachlan ate very little dinner tonight and we are keeping our fingers crossed that this will change soon. Before bedtime I read Lachlan one of the storybooks he had borrowed from the library. It was a book about monsters and he seemed to really enjoy it. After the story we talked about monsters and I asked him if he had ever seen one as I was curious about what his reaction would be. He nodded very decisively that he had seen one. When I told him that I did not think so, he nodded again and started laughing. I told him I thought that perhaps it was Itsal he saw and he laughed.

Lachlan's lips looked red and sore, perhaps from playing outside in the cold windy weather. Lachlan started rubbing them after I applied some moisturiser. I asked him to stop rubbing his lips, explaining that rubbing would them would make them sorer. Lachlan signed the "Crying" sign which meant he was sad, and I was unsure whether it was because his lips were sore or because I had asked him not to rub them.

Friday 19/06/15

Today was the last school day of the term and Lachlan seemed excited. The children needed to wear yellow clothes to school today so Lachlan wore a T-shirt with yellow characters on it. He chose his new black running shoes to wear to school instead of the usual white ones.

Once upon a time Lachlan could not have worn different clothes to school as he was ruled by the routine of wearing the uniform, and changing this part of the routine would have disturbed him. He would not have wanted to change his usual shoes either but these days Lachlan is happy to wear new clothes and shoes.

This evening Lachlan fell asleep after I held his hand for forty minutes. Lachlan will often fall asleep in less time, although sometimes it can take an hour or longer. Itsal is usually on his mat in Lachlan's room and as soon as I leave the room Itsal leaps onto Lachlan's bed and sleeps there for the rest of the night. Tonight Itsal wanted to get onto Lachlan's bed right away even before I left the room. There is always a reason for Itsal's behaviour, but I was unsure why he wanted to join Lachlan earlier tonight. Perhaps he could sense that Lachlan was restless.

Saturday 20/06/15

This morning around 3.00 a.m. Itsal came into our room. I could not hear Lachlan awake as no noises were coming from his room. When I went into Lachlan's room to investigate I saw that Lachlan was still asleep. I stayed in his room for a while wondering why Itsal had woken me as nothing seemed to be out of the ordinary. Ten minutes later while I was still in his room, Lachlan woke up very unwell, and vomited. Somehow Itsal sensed Lachlan was unwell.

Lachlan spent the morning lying in bed too sick to be interested in watching DVDs and hid underneath his pillow. He managed to drink a bottle of juice and kept it down, but did not eat breakfast. Eventually he got out of bed to play on the computer and he seemed a lot better as the morning progressed.

Today was Pastor Guy's 50th Birthday party at church and we were invited. We went along and the party was held in the garden which Lachlan was very familiar with as the church grounds are also the playground of the preschool Lachlan attended as a toddler. The preschool and church are side by side. Lachlan did not seem sick anymore as he ran around the playground happily.

Itsal was a big hit at the party of course as he sat obediently and kept his eye on Lachlan while he played. After around two hours of being at the party I noticed Lachlan was sitting very still. He signed "Finished" and I knew this meant he felt unwell and wanted to go home. Once we returned home Lachlan lay on his bed and rested quietly.

Monday 22/06/15

Today was the first day of school holidays and Lachlan enjoyed sleeping in late, watching DVDs and playing on the computer. We went to the bakery where Lachlan was happy to see his friend Hong who bakes his favourite bread rolls. Next we went to the library and the park and

Lachlan had a short turn on the swing but as he did not want to stay very long, we left.

This afternoon Lachlan pulled out two PECS pictures from his communication folder. One was of Thomas the tank Engine and the other a photo of one of his favourite local shopping centres. Being unsure what he meant by this, I assumed he wanted to buy a Thomas the Tank Engine DVD. Once in the car he directed us to a particular shopping centre, which until very recently he would not have gone anywhere near.

Once inside the shopping centre Lachlan headed to the floor where the children's rides were placed. Once we there I noticed a new Thomas the Tank Engine ride which had not been there on our last visit. Lachlan was very excited and now we knew what he had meant. He wanted to go to the shops and see the Thomas the Tank Engine ride. We wondered how he knew the new ride would be there. One of those mysteries. Somehow he seemed to know it would be.

We wondered if the rides were rotated within the shopping centre as those are the kinds of things he would remember even if nobody else would. Lachlan has an excellent memory and seems to remember patterns and cycles.

Tuesday 23/06/15

Itsal woke me this morning as I had slept in and he needed the toilet. Lachlan was still asleep but Itsal could not wait any longer. When it was time to feed Itsal I noticed he sat and did not eat his food. He looked at me as though I was crazy and when I asked him to eat his food, and was reluctant. Eventually I realised the reason for Itsal's reluctance was that I had once again not fed our cat first which was usual for the morning routine. After I realised this was the reason, I reassured Itsal and he ate his food.

Today we had planned to go to the movies. I reminded Lachlan of our plans and he seemed pleased. He had a good experience last time we went to the movies so I thought he would be happy to go again. When we were ready to go, Itsal was waiting patiently at the door, looking forward to the outing. Lachlan pulled out his PECS communication folder and selected three cards. The first one was 'Thomas the tank Engine', the second one was 'shop', and the third one was 'DVD'. Thinking that he would enjoy the movies once we arrived, I suggested movies again. Lachlan was quite determined that he wanted to go the shops and not the movies, and he had selected the same shopping centre as yesterday.

Once we arrived at the shopping centre Lachlan headed straight for the Thomas the Tank Engine ride again. Two boys were riding on it and Lachlan enjoyed watching them having fun. When they finished their ride Lachlan was still busy watching it. He did not want to have a ride himself, he just wanted to watch.

Next he wanted to go to and look at DVDs. He selected five, but eventually settled for one. He was quite happy waiting in the line to buy it and afterwards took it out of the bag and carried it around the shopping centre. Next he chose a muffin and we sat down at a table while Lachlan ate his muffin and opened his new DVD to take a better look at it.

After that Lachlan signed "Finished" and I knew this meant he wanted to go home. I told him we needed to go to the supermarket first as I needed to buy some groceries, and he agreed to follow me there. Once we were inside Lachlan saw some bread rolls he liked the look of and wanted to buy them, and after we got the other items we needed we headed back to the car and drove home.

It was totally amazing to see Lachlan walking around this shopping centre, happy and confident like he was today. This particular shopping centre had caused a huge amount of anxiety before Itsal came along. Not only would he not enter this particular shopping centre, we could not even drive past it or head in the same direction as it. Lachlan would become completely anxious and stressed being anywhere near it. Lachlan had an occupational therapist who had suggested just walking past the shopping centre at first as a good start. It was really amazing to see him enjoying the shopping centre the same as most other children, even though the shops were quite busy. Lachlan was not bothered at all by the noise or crowd.

No longer is it necessary for me to trace Lachlan's foot onto a piece of paper in order to buy shoes for him at the shopping centre (well, maybe for convenience sake). He is now able to go into the shoe shop, which is fantastic. What a huge step forward for him and what a lot of enjoyment he will get from exploring different shops.

Wednesday 24/06/15

Today we went to another local shopping centre which I thought Lachlan would enjoy as it has many children's rides. Once we arrived at the entrance, Lachlan hid his face under my arm and I knew it was because he was reluctant to enter the shopping centre. I encouraged him to hold onto Itsal's harness, which he did. As I kept on walking toward the shopping centre, Lachlan focussed on Itsal and seemed to forget his fear of entering the shopping centre.

Once we were inside he became excited and he pointed to the direction he wanted us to follow. He had been to this shopping centre before and remembered where all of his favourite rides and shops were. While walking ahead Lachlan was very excited to come across a stand filled with DVDs. He looked at some of them but did not seem particularly interested in any. Lachlan then forged ahead with something else in mind which he wanted to see. I was unsure what it was, but followed his lead to the end of the shopping centre.

He led me to a children's train ride which looked like a small merry-go-round and Lachlan started to jump up and down with excitement when he saw it. Next he put some money into the ride and as it turned around he decided to stand on its platform. A boy around four years old and his mother came near and the mother told me that her son had seen Itsal from a distance and wanted to come closer to see him. The boy was not interested in the train ride like Lachlan was, he was only interested in Itsal. The boy's mother told me that her son adored dogs and then asked Lachlan for permission to pat Itsal. Lachlan nodded in agreement. We should really have said no, but agreed as a one off.

Strangely enough, the little boy was then reluctant to pat Itsal which surprised his mother. He just wanted to look. He stayed for a while looking at Itsal while his mother chatted with me. While chatting I kept my eye on Lachlan and the ride. It is not unusual for us to run off in the middle of a conversation if we need to attend to Lachlan.

I am sure that many parents of children with autism would understand exactly what I mean by this. It is just the way it goes. I have heard other parents of children with autism say that they felt relieved when they spoke to people who understood this, that if they needed to run off mid-conversation that would be fine. As it worked out today, I did not need to do this.

When we did the dog handler training at Righteous Pups Australia we were relieved that the staff and other parents understood this. The staff at Righteous Pups Australia were understanding warm-hearted people who just seemed to know the limitations Lachlan and the rest of the family often faced. They genuinely wanted to help the families through their trained assistance dogs and paid special attention to the siblings of the children who had received their assistance dog by providing them with their own trained assistance dog for the duration of the training to participate with their sibling.

On the first day of the training when Lachlan met Itsal he did not seem very interested in him and ran off to play by himself while Itsal stayed behind with me. Three other families who were also being trained met up with their Righteous Pups at the same time.

We were a little concerned that Lachlan and Itsal did not bond straight away. Lachlan even seemed a little scared of Itsal, especially of his face. Lachlan avoided Itsal's face and would sit or stand at the back of him only, as I think he was concerned about Itsal licking him.

Joanne and Jenny from Righteous Pups Australia assured us that Lachlan would get used to Itsal. They told us they had seen the same situation before resolving itself successfully. It was very helpful to hear that.

Slowly Lachlan became used to being with Itsal, and the third day of the training with Righteous Pups

Australia there was a breakthrough. Lachlan lay on the floor and looked into Itsal's face intently. Joanne and Jenny looked over at him while they spoke during the training and we all knew things had changed. Lachlan and Itsal started to form a bond from then on.

As part of the training we went to various shopping centres, parks and reserves. We went to a soccer game, a restaurant, a cafe and the local library. We also went on train ride into the country which was Lachlan's favourite day and the bond between Lachlan and Itsal grew stronger every day.

As well as the trips into the community with the Righteous Pups Australia team, we had training on how to read the body language of other dogs which we found very helpful should we need to identify potential threats to Itsal. We learned about first aid for dogs and hazards such as poisonous foods and plants for dogs and much more.

We practised all the commands over and over daily until we were confident handlers and it was extremely exciting when Itsal was able to come and stay with us at our accommodation in Bendigo.

Lachlan and Itsal's bond was becoming stronger but as yet Lachlan was not ready to have Itsal sleep in the same room so I took Itsal into our room and he lay on a mat next to the bed. I got into bed and when Chris entered the room later on in the evening, Itsal growled at him and was clearly unhappy about him being there. He decided to sleep in the other room.

Back at the training the next day we discussed how Itsal had growled at Chris the night before and Joanne and Jen said that Itsal and Chris had not formed a strong bond as yet. The reason was that while the training was happening Chris had taken Lachlan in and out of the training room which gave him a chance to run around outside as Lachlan has never liked to sit for long periods. The staff at Righteous Pups Australia understood Lachlan's needs. As Chris was in the training room for less time than myself, the bond between him and Itsal was weaker than the bond between Itsal and myself. Before long the bond between Lachlan and Itsal would become the strongest one of all.

Back at the shops this afternoon, Lachlan walked around and looked at all the other rides. We bought some groceries and Lachlan chose some hot dog rolls (which he had never eaten before) and I was very pleased he was interested in them. Lachlan helped put the items onto the counter, except the vegetables which he was not going to touch, no way!

Thursday 25/06/15

Lachlan awoke at 3.00 am and was awake until around 6.00 a.m. when he fell asleep again after being given his DVD player. He slept for a few more hours. This morning a respite carer was coming to meet Lachlan for the first time. She may take Lachlan on an outing eventually when Lachlan knows her and feels comfortable, but for now the three of us planned to go to the local shops and the park for the morning.

It is going to take time for both of us having someone else to take Lachlan out as he has only ever been out with his immediate family before. As well as family, three lovely family friends; Linda, Joan and Pamela have cared for Lachlan occasionally before.

Lachlan has only ever had one respite carer before, Pamela who has been coming for five years now. Lachlan likes her very much and we all trust Pamela. She has such a lot of warmth and kindness towards Lachlan and he is always so happy to see her. Lachlan often starts dancing around whenever he sees her.

This afternoon Lachlan played in his sandpit and then he and Itsal amused themselves with a game of fetch with a stick. Lachlan was amazed when he saw how fast Itsal could run while playing. Itsal ran circles around Lachlan very fast, but was able to slow himself down just at the right time so that he did not bump into Lachlan. For a large animal, Itsal displayed excellent control over his body. He is not the slightest bit clumsy. His movements as usual were very precise.

After lunch Lachlan went to the cupboard where the cleaning products are stored and removed a bottle of car washing liquid and two sponges which indicated what he wanted to do during the afternoon. He must have noticed the few dirty spots on the car this morning. While I filled up the bucket with warm water to clean the car, Lachlan signed "More" as he wanted more water after I turned off the tap. I then filled the bucket entirely and wondered how I would carry such a heavy bucket down the stairs and outside to the car.

When I attempted to lift it, Lachlan tried to help and I could not believe that he picked up the full bucket easily and carried it down the stairs by himself. I half expected him to drop it but he is very strong and carried it easily.

Lachlan enjoyed washing the car, one section at a time. He made sure all the dirty marks had been cleaned off and he did not miss any as he is a perfectionist. Next he hosed the car down and his clothes became wet, which did not bother him.

Friday 26/06/15

Today we went to another set of shops where there were some of Lachlan's favourite children's rides. We had also planned to buy some new toys for Itsal. When we arrived Lachlan became a little upset as we were unable find a parking spot immediately. It took around five minutes until a space became available and Lachlan was happy once again. We went into Lachlan's chosen shop and found the dog toys and Lachlan started laughing when I pressed an unusual looking toy which made a squeaking sound. When I asked him if he thought Itsal would like it, he laughed even more but pointed to some tennis balls as he knew Itsal would definitely love those.

Next we went to the newsagent to buy a birthday card for Lachlan's cousin. Lachlan started to look around in the newsagent and found a box which contained DVDs. They looked a little outdated and there were various categories such as weddings, fishing, cars, trucks and aeroplanes.

Lachlan picked out a DVD about four-wheel drives, another about a pilot and aeroplanes, and another about racing cars. The woman who worked at the news agency asked Lachlan, "How are you today little man?" and I encouraged Lachlan to sign "Good" by holding up his thumb, which he did. He signed "Thank you" when the shop assistant handed him the DVDs and wanted to go home straight away to watch them.

This afternoon Itsal enjoyed the tennis balls which Lachlan threw to him. Itsal was so excited that it made Lachlan laugh hysterically when he saw him run around in circles with the ball. Before now Lachlan had found it a little difficult to throw balls, but recently his gross motor skills seemed to have improved a lot, which is fantastic.

When we went back inside after the fetch game with Itsal, Lachlan looked in the cupboard where the cleaning products were stored and got out some upholstery cleaner used for the car interior. This time Lachlan wanted to clean the inside of the car.

I encouraged Lachlan to press the spray pump of the upholstery spray bottle which he had not been able to do previously. This time when he tried to press the spray pump he found he could and he went on to clean the interior of the car. He really enjoyed doing this and he also cleaned his bike seat.

Next Lachlan was interested in using window cleaning spray to clean the car windows. He sprayed all the windows and was very pleased that he had found another task he could now do independently. Lachlan would be quite happy to clean the car every day and sometimes he will ask to clean it one day after it had been cleaned already. Lachlan cannot understand why I do not want to clean my car every day.

This afternoon Samantha came over for dinner. I asked Lachlan to pick some mandarins from our tree to give to Samantha. There were about thirty mandarins on the tree and they tasted so much better than any we had bought from a supermarket. Lachlan has never eaten one, but we are working up to that. The first stage is seeing and touching them. He liked picking them from the tree and picked twelve to give to Samantha. When I ate one of the mandarins Lachlan was interested and appalled at the same time. Like many foods, I often wonder if Lachlan would like them if he tasted them.

He was pleased and smiled when Samantha told him she liked the mandarins he picked for her as he liked making her happy. When Samantha left after dinner Lachlan went outside to wave to her along with Itsal, because it was dark. Itsal makes all of us feel safe.

Saturday 27/06/15

Today Lachlan went bushwalking with Dad. Lachlan forged ahead and they walked eight kilometres in total. Lachlan as usual had a lot of energy and did not tire easily. He enjoyed seeing the rapidly changing scenery change as he walked. He walked along various logs he came across and found a huge one with a hollow middle where he sat and ate his lunch. He was interested in birds he saw especially some green finches with red beaks. There were also crows and an eagle he enjoyed looking at. Lachlan liked seeing different plants and pulled some leaves off them at times to feel them. He touched the sandstone walls along the walking track at the bottom of a cliff.

As Lachlan always seems happiest when he has been given the chance to use up his energy, this morning he came home in a very happy mood.

This afternoon in the car Lachlan pointed which indicated the direction he wanted to follow. As we did not have firm plans to go to one place or another I followed his directions. I did not know what he was thinking but I was about to find out. Lachlan led me along various streets for some time and seemed to know where he was going. He was very pleased when we came across a shopping centre we'd never been to before. He did not want to enter this shopping centre but led me to a second shopping centre. He seemed to know the way from the first shopping centre to the second one and I still do not know how he knew this.

Lachlan stood at the front of the second shopping centre for ten minutes and observed shoppers going in and out before he decided to go inside for a look. He seemed very happy to have made his way to this second shopping centre. Once inside he looked around the shops before he led Itsal and I back to the first shopping centre where he had a quick look at some shop windows and wanted to go home.

This would have been unthinkable before Itsal came as it would have been far too stressful for him. These days, no problem. Amazing!

Sunday 28/06/15

Lachlan went bike riding today. Firstly he rode to the shops, as there was a children's ride he wanted to look at, then he rode to a park and then another park which had a bike track. After a turn on the swing at the second park he rode onto the bike track. He steered well and seemed to remember the skill even though it has been some time since he last rode his bike. It can be quite scary to watch him as he rides fast and we need to run fast to keep up with him. He can ride long distances without becoming even the least bit tired. Sometimes I need to stop him so that I can catch my breath and that makes him laugh.

Monday 29/06/15

The first thing that happened this morning was that Lachlan played ball with Itsal. Lachlan was not keen on taking the ball from Itsal's mouth as it was wet with his saliva but after a while he decided to take it from Itsal's mouth. Lachlan threw the ball and when Itsal retrieved it, I asked him to sit so that Lachlan could take the ball from his mouth. After we did this a few times I was surprised and excited when Itsal retrieved the ball and Lachlan said the word "Sit" to him. This was the first time Lachlan had spoken the word "Sit". How wonderful!

Lachlan and I went the local shops to look at the rides, and then across the road to the park where Lachlan had a turn on the swing. He usually gestures for me to push him, but today he pushed himself using his legs. Itsal laid on the ground without me holding his lead as I needed to stay close to Lachlan on the swing. Itsal knew even without a command that we needed him to wait right where he was. This particular park is one of Lachlan's favourites as it is very small and usually has just a few people at it, or no one else.

This afternoon we went to another park which was bigger and better one than the one we visited this morning. From the car Lachlan could see the park was quite crowded which made him reluctant to leave it. Just as I was about to turn around and drive back home, Lachlan jumped out of the car and walked towards the park. The park had a walking and riding track as well as swings, a slide and climbing equipment. When Lachlan had a turn on the swing he signed for "More" several times which meant he wanted to go higher and higher. Quite amazing that he did not fall off the swing as he held a muffin in one hand, and did not always hold onto the swing with his other hand.

He loved watching the other children ride their scooters. Today everyone seemed to have scooters. Lachlan likes his scooter also, but needs some support to ride it, unlike his bike which he rides independently. Lachlan played on the park equipment where some younger-looking boys also played. One of them said to Lachlan "What are you looking at?" Lachlan responded by going up close to the boy and tapping him on the head. The boy stood there, frozen. Lachlan was a lot bigger than him, and I think he realised now that Lachlan was not frightened at all. The boy and his friends left straight away and Lachlan went on playing by himself.

Tuesday 30/06/15

Itsal came and woke me sometime before 6.00 a.m. by nudging my arm. Just as he did, I heard Lachlan walking around in his room and I could hear music coming from his musical aquarium. The morning routine began with Lachlan seeking out his DVD player and a DVD to watch.

With some errands to run, we visited the local shopping centre. Lachlan wanted to look in the newsagent as he remembered the box of DVDs they sold there. Lachlan selected one on sport, fishing and one on weddings from the collection of DVDs about various subjects. Last time we visited Lachlan was also interested in the wedding DVD but I encouraged him to look at others which I thought he may have preferred. He had decided he definitely wanted the wedding DVD and I wondered what it was about it that interested him. When I looked at it later I found it showed how to create wedding stationery. Maybe Lachlan liked the idea of making something.

In the afternoon, we went for a walk along the bike track at the park. Lachlan started running and ran extremely fast. I was very glad that I had his backpack with me which meant I could place everything inside it and run along with him. He ran so fast that I needed to stop him twice so that I could catch up. When he was younger he would not have stopped running in the same situation, which is another positive change I have noted as Lachlan grows older.

Lachlan had a turn on the swing and had been swinging for around fifteen minutes before a little girl walked up to him and asked for a turn on the swing. Her friend sat on the swing next to Lachlan. I suggested to Lachlan that the girl should have a turn on the swing and he got up and went and sat on another swing. This, too, Lachlan would not have done when he was younger. He would have had a meltdown about having to share the swing.

Lachlan approached some children at the park as he wanted to play with them. There were five children and three of them ran away (maybe because Lachlan was so much bigger than them). Of the two children who remained one boy seemed very interested in Lachlan and started following him around. Lachlan was pleased and amused at having made a friend to play with.

Chapter 7
July 2015

Thursday 02/07/15

Lachlan chose his favourite local shops to visit today, and the shopping centre was busy as usual for the school holiday period. Lachlan looked at some toys and found a dinosaur he seemed particularly interested in which he played with for a while, and next he looked at some DVDs. He never tires of looking at DVDs. When we were on our way out of the store Lachlan noticed someone dressed as a superhero. There was new brand of toothpaste being launched and he was the toothpaste superhero. Lachlan seemed excited and fascinated, so approached him and observed his masked face. Next he touched his pointy plastic cheeks. Lachlan knew they were too good to be true.

Next Lachlan tried to touch the superhero's teeth. He knew there was no way those perfect shiny teeth could have been real. There were two girls also involved in promoting the toothpaste and they could not stop laughing as they watched Lachlan interact with the superhero.

Next he touched the superhero's huge cheeks again and this time he squeezed them. Another little boy who seemed very interested watched on, perhaps because he wondered the same things. Lachlan went back to the superhero's teeth again but the superhero waved goodbye to Lachlan as he needed to leave. Lachlan would have been happy to stay longer and figure out which things were real and which things were not.

Back at home during the afternoon Lachlan and Itsal played fetch with a tennis ball. Itsal ran around and around in circles as fast as he could. Lachlan stepped back out of the way as Itsal ran so fast, laughing hysterically as Itsal's running threw up little patches of grass.

Friday 03/07/15

Today Lachlan and I had some grocery shopping to do. Lachlan wanted to go to a different and bigger shopping centre to look at DVDs and rides, so he was not entirely happy with my choice today. After I wrote a shopping list, I showed it to him and read out the items. Lachlan nodded to show me that he understood what needed to be done.

Once we were inside the grocery store, I asked Lachlan to pick out four sweet potatoes, or kumara as some people call it. One by one he flung them into the trolley. There was a woman nearby who started to laugh when she saw Lachlan tossing the sweet potatoes and she came over talk to him. "You're a bit rough on those sweet potatoes matey," she said, and Lachlan went over to her and grabbed onto her arm and cuddled into it. The woman suggested that Lachlan could put the sweet potatoes into a bag and when I got one, he did put them inside the bag. Next he reached for some mandarins as at home he often picks them from our tree. I told Lachlan that we did not need any mandarins and he threw it down which made it break open. The woman who had been chatting to Lachlan saw that he had thrown the mandarin and said to me, "Can't little boys be naughty sometimes? I have three and they were all like that."

After we found all the items on the list we headed to the checkout. Lachlan was very helpful and loaded most of the groceries onto the counter while the worker chatted to him. Most of the people at the shop know Lachlan and Itsal and they usually chat to Lachlan. Lachlan nodded in response to the worker's questions and vocalised at times. He likes it when people talk to him, most of the time that is.

We had set up a table-tennis table in the garage for Lachlan to play this afternoon but he was more interested in playing fetch with Itsal today. Itsal liked it too.

Saturday 04/07/15

Lachlan had his first ever sleep over at Samantha's house which would be his first night away without a parent. We all agreed that Samantha's house would be perfect for Lachlan's first sleepover. I made a social story which explained the sleepover to Lachlan and the activities likely to happen there. Lachlan became very excited and could not wait for Samantha to arrive. He organised his favourite toys to take as well as his pillow while he waited for Samantha to arrive. He held onto his favourite DVDs which he would take with him to watch at Samantha's house.

As soon as Samantha arrived with her friend, Lachlan took hold of Itsal's harness and wanted to leave right away. He was not reluctant at all about going to Samantha's house. He swiftly took his spot in the back seat of her car with Itsal in his usual place on the right-hand side of Lachlan, and off they went for the night.

During the evening I heard that Lachlan watched a DVD and enjoyed running around in the garage with Itsal and Honey, Samantha's dog. Lachlan slept well overnight and only became a little upset when Samantha and Lachlan arrived back home and I had not yet returned from my shopping trip. Lachlan cried but when Samantha told him I was on my way home, he stopped crying. When I returned five minutes later, Lachlan was pleased. When I asked him about the sleepover he seemed very proud of himself. I think he liked being independent.

Monday 06/07/15

This morning we had a surprise visit from our friend Linda whom we had not seen for some time. It was lovely to see her again. Linda was Lachlan's preschool special need support educator and we have remained friends. After Linda and I chatted for a short time, Lachlan approached her and sat on her lap which reminded me of how excited he always was when he went to preschool. We were sure that Mrs Linda was one of the reasons he enjoyed it so much. Linda and the other staff were always so kind to him and he loved all the fun activities. It was a fantastic preschool in every way.

Linda also played a huge part in Lachlan receiving Itsal. Linda and I first discussed assistance dogs after we both saw a television segment on Autism Assistance Dogs by Righteous Pups Australia. We both knew Lachlan would benefit from having one of these amazing dogs and we were all thrilled when his application was accepted. Linda and her family started to do fundraising for Righteous Pups Australia as volunteers and arranged and held various fundraising events. Linda also set up a fundraising team which was called Team L. Linda, Ken, Danielle, Tommy, Toni, Leigh, Chris and Gill helped run and organise fundraising events. There were many high teas and a dinner dance party which were so much fun and Linda did a huge amount of work to make sure they all ran perfectly. Linda's children Danielle and Tommy also held fundraising events as well as the preschool Lachlan had attended as a toddler.

Our local church held various fundraising events and Karen came up with the brilliant idea of "Harry the helper" which were little stuffed toy dogs sewn by herself and some other talented church members which were sold to support the fundraising.

All of these people did an amazing job supporting Righteous Pups Australia and Lachlan as they worked many long hours and we could never thank them enough.

While Linda and I chatted during the morning she was also excited when I told her that Lachlan had planned to try out the surf simulator this Thursday. She offered to come along with us which Lachlan and I were very pleased about. Lachlan has shown a keen interest in learning to surf for some time and if the trial goes well we hoped to arrange some regular lessons.

This afternoon Lachlan requested a visit to the large shopping centre where his favourite rides and DVDs were. When we arrived it was quite crowded and it took some time before we found a parking space. Lachlan was not disturbed while we waited to park although when he was younger this would have bothered him a great deal.

Today Lachlan was to have dental work performed under general anaesthetic. He needed X-rays, crowns, teeth sealing and other work. For the last ten days we've practiced using a facemask with a mask which I bought from the pharmacy to simulate the genuine experience of using a facemask. We took turns using it each day and Lachlan accepted his turn of holding the mask to his face.

To help prepare Lachlan for the dental work I made a social story with pictures which started with a picture of the hospital. The social story counts down the days (a bit like what children like to do at Christmas time). We started the countdown five days before and the story read, "This is the hospital where Lachlan will go to have his teeth fixed in five days". On the next page there is a picture of his juice bottle and it said, "Lachlan will have his juice at the hospital with some special medicine in it". On the third page there was a picture of myself with the practice mask on my face and it said, "I will use a mask like this one and we can count, nineteen, eighteen, seventeen down to number one, then Lachlan will go to sleep and doctor will fix Lachlan's teeth" On the next page there was a picture of the doctor who would do the dental work who Lachlan had visited previously. On the fifth page there was a picture of Lachlan's family and the story told him that while he was asleep his family would be there. The sixth page had a picture of a present and said, "When Lachlan wakes up he will have a present".

The last page had a picture of a big white smile and said, "Lachlan's teeth will be healthy and beautiful".

Lachlan was fully prepared for the procedure. At the hospital, he was given some sedation medication mixed in with his usual juice in his usual bottle but when he tasted its bitterness he was quite determined that he was not going to drink it, no way!

The doctor told us it did not matter very much that Lachlan had rejected the medication as many of the children did the same. I knew that Lachlan would be more willing to use the mask for sedation as he is highly sensitive to taste.

Next we took Lachlan into the room where he had the procedure. He did not seem bothered by the surgical equipment in the room. There were around five people in the room. He happily sat on the bed but was a little reluctant to lay down at first. He did lay down and Dad had a turn of using the plastic mask from the pharmacy. While the doctor prepared the mask for Lachlan I told him that he and I would have a turn at the same time. As we did this I began to count down from twenty just like we had practised. When Lachlan realised he was becoming drowsy, he tried to push the mask away. After we counted down to zero Lachlan was still awake so we started counting down again until the medication had taken effect and Lachlan fell asleep. I quickly left the room and wanted the procedure to be over as soon as possible. So far all was going well.

Even though I knew Lachlan was in good hands, I wanted to go outside and away from the hospital, if not somewhere (anywhere) far away, until I heard that the procedure was over and that all was well.

We went out into the street and had coffee and when we returned to the hospital the nurse told us that Lachlan was waking up and invited us to his bedside. He stirred as the nurse told us he still had a cannula in his hand. Lachlan was half asleep and tried to take the net off his hand which held the cannula in place. The nurse then removed the cannula and I think Lachlan was pleased about that. He continued to stir and seemed slightly angry and very confused.

The nurses were worried that Lachlan would hit his head as he began to thrash from side to side a few times, so they assisted him to sit in a recliner. The nurses wheeled the recliner out into a small room where Lachlan enjoyed watching cartoons on the television there. He fell asleep on and off for the next two hours.

In the meantime both doctors came to see how Lachlan was doing, which was well. Lachlan had a good outcome as no extractions were needed, just preventative treatment. After around two hours he had some juice and the nurses told us he could go home when he was ready. He was calm now and nodded when asked if he was ready to go home. So off we went with Lachlan in a wheelchair to the entrance. He enjoyed the ride.

The doctors and staff were very respectful to Lachlan and we are very grateful they were happy to do what worked best for him. The procedure ran very smoothly.

Wednesday 08/07/15

Lachlan seemed not quite himself today. He appeared a little tired but still wanted to go out. He went and watched a string quartet perform at a cathedral in the city, as he loves classical music. There were four people playing violins which Lachlan really liked. He focused on the way the musicians played their instruments and it captured his interest so much that we wondered if he would leave his seat and approach them. The more he listened the more excited he became and then found it hard to sit in his seat as he wanted to dance around. Occasionally I noticed he stared off into the distance while he concentrated on the music. When he became restless we went window shopping at some nearby shops.

Lachlan stumbled upon classical music one day as he walked past a church where there was a wedding in progress. He insisted on going inside where a string quartet was playing. Since that day he likes to check inside churches as he walks past as he never knows what exciting things he may find.

Today was a very exciting day as it was Lachlan's first surfing lesson on the surf simulator at the swim centre. He was so excited and if it goes as well as expected hopefully he will be able to start regular surfing lessons. Last week I spoke to Leah who kindly offered Lachlan an opportunity to try out the simulator alone before other children started their sessions during the school holiday program.

Lachlan is very familiar with this particular swim centre and he loves swimming there. He likes the different pools, especially the wave pool with simulated waves. He likes to swim at the deep end so that when the alarm sounds and the waves start, he can make the most of them with the water swishing and pulling him upwards so that he can no longer touch the bottom of the pool.

Yesterday I made a social story on Lachlan's iPad which included a video of the surf simulator. Lachlan played it over and over as he loved the idea. He was so excited that he continued to play it all the way in the car until the battery went flat just before we arrived at the pool. Linda and I found this amusing.

Leah mentioned that the simulator was noisy and some of the children did not like the noise it made. Lachlan put his fingers in his ears when it first started up, but after a minute or two he uncovered his ears when he saw all the water flowing, because he was excited.

Lachlan jumped up and down with excitement when the water flowed from the simulator and flooded the mat. It was soft to stand on, and he liked it straight away.

The water in the simulator was heated so it was only the night air which felt slightly cold. I was surprised about this as I had expected it to feel much colder. A wetsuit could be used to help keep warm if necessary in the future.

Lachlan laughed as he walked through the warm flowing water and I could see he was having the time of his life. An instructor showed Lachlan how to lay and stand on the board. Lachlan wanted to stand on it and surf and he was not at all frightened to try. He stood on the board while it was held it in place. He did this a few times. What a great start!

Leah gave the right instructions for the lesson to proceed as it should and Linda, Leah and myself watched as the instructor held onto the board while Lachlan held his shoulders to steady himself. Linda noticed that Lachlan appeared to have hurt his foot on the mat which made him want to stop the lesson temporarily. Nothing serious, perhaps he had stubbed his toe. He had a fantastic time and he did extremely well for his first lesson. I had no doubt that Lachlan could learn to surf.

Afterwards, Linda and I chatted to Leah while Lachlan walked around the pool. Leah and I discussed that the iPad could be used to explain the goals for the lesson and I thought that was a great idea. Linda helped

Lachlan change into dry clothes while I chatted to Leah. Leah would seek out a possible instructor for Lachlan and set a firm day and time, and she would let me know next week after she had spoken to the people she needed to. Fingers crossed! Leah spent a lot of time with us today, which we were very grateful for and we could hardly wait to see what she would arrange for Lachlan.

Friday 10/07/15

Today was Mathew's birthday. Mathew was Lachlan's cousin and he would have been twenty-eight years old today. Mathew passed away in 2013, two years ago. Lachlan and I had bought some flowers on the way to visit his memorial. When we arrived Lachlan was reluctant to get out of the car at first and as we walked towards the memorial I could see Lachlan's uncle and Mathew's grandmother sitting there talking to each other.

Earlier in the day I had explained to Lachlan that we planned to visit Mathew's memorial and I showed him a photo of Mathew to jog his memory. The photo that was handy showed Mathew as a child. When Lachlan saw it I didn't think he recognised it as the Mathew he knew, as Lachlan only knew him as an adult after the tragic car accident which meant he needed to use a wheelchair and be fed through a tube.

Maybe it was best that Lachlan did not recognise Mathew from the school photo I had shown him as I had never spoken specifically to him about Mathew's passing. I was unsure at the time of Mathew's passing whether Lachlan would have understood the concept or if he would have expected Mathew to be at the memorial park in his wheelchair, just as Lachlan remembered him. Lachlan loved his cousin and I am sure he misses him, but I remain unsure whether he links the memorial park together with Mathew.

The way Lachlan and Mathew interacted before Mathew passed away was something really special. Mathew often held Lachlan when he was a baby which always made him smile. As Lachlan grew he would bounce Mathew's wheelchair vigorously while he sat in it which made Mathew laugh and they formed a strong relationship without either communicating verbally. Lachlan had never known Mathew to be any different.

Without the social context, the memorial park was really just a giant park. Lachlan ran around and was interested in decorations people had placed on their loved one's memorials. His Uncle Jim supervised him while I chatted to Mathew's grandmother. Uncle Jim asked Lachlan not to touch the ornaments, and he did as he was asked. Lachlan sat and played with some rocks he had found instead.

That afternoon Lachlan's friends Erin and Saxon came to visit along with their mother, Trish, who is a long-time friend of the family. Lachlan did not interact with Erin and Saxon very much as he was busy with his

DVDs. I remembered a few years ago when Erin visited, she had said "Hi" to Lachlan and he replied with a clear "Hi" back. Another time Erin offered him a biscuit and I could not believe he accepted it and ate it. That was the first time he had ever eaten that particular type of biscuit, which was a big deal for Lachlan.

It is a major step when Lachlan tries a new food. Erin had an expectation that he would eat the biscuit, as she didn't know how unusual it was for Lachlan to try new foods. It seemed like he rose to meet her expectation. Now I just need Erin to come and live at my house!

Later that evening after Trish and the children had gone home; I noticed Lachlan was looking in the mirror with his mouth open checking out the new silver crowns on his teeth. He noticed how different they looked and they probably felt very different, too, but I think he liked them.

Saturday 11/07/15

Today we had tickets for a steam train ride and train museum which Lachlan had visited previously. He was thrilled to ride the steam train again and of course Itsal was a big hit with all the other passengers.

Lachlan was invited to sit next to the driver's cabin which was the perfect place for him to eat his lunch. He was very happy with the great view he had.

Sunday 12/07/15

Today Lachlan's soccer team were mascots for the A Grade team. Lachlan proudly wore the medal that he won some weeks ago. Whenever Lachlan has seen a soccer, rugby league or cricket game being played he has always wanted to be involved. At times he has run onto sporting fields in the middle of games. Some players thought it was very funny, but then we would have to remove him from their game. This time it was Lachlan's turn to run onto the field and Lachlan was very eager to be involved.

On arriving at the venue Lachlan needed to wait in a cocktail lounge before crossing the car park onto the oval. He watched the end of a soccer game being played by some teenagers before he was called over to go into the wire tunnel where the players entered and exited the field. Next, the players from the previous game came out and gave the kids a 'high five'. Lachlan was so excited.

The A Grade players came out into the tunnel next and Lachlan was very pleased to get more 'high fives' from four of them. Next the A Grade players lined up in the tunnel beside Lachlan and the other children. Then the tunnel opened and everyone ran out to line up in front of the stand. Lachlan was extremely happy and was laughing and smiling. First he started off running slow and became faster and faster until he was sprinting on the field.

While running, one of the A Grade players linked arms with Lachlan to run to the right spot on the field. Once they were there Lachlan stood in front of the line and jumped up and down as he was so excited. When the game started the children ran forward and out of the gate. After exiting through the gate, Lachlan wanted to watch the game so he went and sat in the stand.

Monday 13/07/15

Today was the last day of school holidays and we planned to go to the movies. The movie Lachlan wanted to see was not screening in our local area so we drove to the suburb where the movie screened which was inside a shopping centre. The drive took forty minutes and I had not been to this shopping centre before. When we arrived Lachlan seemed relaxed, and I assumed he had probably visited the shopping centre before with Dad, given that he seemed so calm. Something that once seemed impossible due to the sensory overload Lachlan experienced in unfamiliar and sometimes familiar shopping centres.

Lachlan seemed excited when he saw all the shops and Itsal knew exactly what he needed to do. We looked around for the cinema, but we couldn't see it at first. Then I noticed an employee of the centre walking around and asked him where the cinema was. He told me it was in the next building and when I suggested to Lachlan that we go there, he pointed at the shops. He had changed his mind about the movie it seemed, so we decided to take a look around the shopping centre instead. He led the way along with Itsal around the shopping centre, and I was sure he had something in mind which he wanted to see as he seemed to know where he was going.

We walked up, down and around as Lachlan charged ahead and he stopped when he came to a children's ride he liked. He put some money into the slot and stood on the ride as it turned around and he enjoyed the music which came from it. I thought Lachlan had found what he had been looking for when he rushed ahead, but when the ride finished he had something else in mind and dashed ahead toward it. We went up some stairs and around some corners and then he led Itsal and myself out of the main part of the shopping centre to another section which was outside. Lachlan still charged ahead and seemed to know exactly where to go. Then we came to another children's ride, and I guessed it must have been what he was looking for. Some children played on the ride so Lachlan happily watched them as they enjoyed themselves.

The children's ride was next to a fruit market so I took the opportunity to go inside and buy a few items. Lachlan and Itsal waited patiently while I found the items I needed and Lachlan helped by placing some avocados and bananas in bags. Once we were at the checkout counter, the woman working there was very interested in Itsal started to ask some questions about him. As I chatted with her, Itsal noticed that Lachlan had moved closer to the shop exit and pulled me away to follow him. Thank you, Itsal.

Lachlan then pointed in the direction he wanted us to follow. He led us out of this shopping centre and into another shopping centre and I was unsure whether it was part of the same centre or not. We went up, down and around and by this time I now wondered how I would find the way back to the car. Embarrassing as it was at the time, I had lost the car once before when Lachlan was much younger.

Lachlan found the third children's ride and stood on it as it went around in circles. Next he went into a shop which sold DVDs to take a look at their collection. We looked in a few other shops before Lachlan signed the "Finished" sign and wanted to go home. Now we needed to find the car. Thankfully, I remembered part of the route we had walked so we went back to the other shopping centre which was outdoors and into another section of shops where we were previously. Next I wondered whether to turn left or right as I tried to recall if any of the shops looked familiar, but they didn't.

Hoping that Lachlan would not become distressed, I told him we were going back to the car and as we walked I tried to figure out the right way back. Lachlan pointed to an exit on his left but when we got close to it, it did not look familiar at all. I told him, "No, not that way", as I did not know where that exit led, and it seemed to lead onto the street when we needed to find the carpark. Lachlan insisted as he pointed to the left street exit again. I told him it was time to go home as I thought he still must have wanted to look in other shops.

He pointed once again to the left exit and became a little upset, so I decided to follow him, hoping we were not getting even further away from the car park. We went outside onto the street and around a corner where there was a different entrance to a section of the shops. We went inside, up, down and around, and we were now back at our original spot where we had first entered the shops some time ago. Now I knew where we were and the way to get back to the car park. Amazing how Lachlan knew this different way to get back to the car park even though it was not the same way we came.

I thought for sure Lachlan must have been familiar with this particular set of shops but the strange thing was that when I asked Dad he said that he and Lachlan had never been there before except for once when they had tried to go there and Lachlan would not get out of the car so they did not go inside. This was before Itsal came as Lachlan would not visit shopping centres previously. I then wondered how Lachlan knew about the rides and their locations. He didn't seem to just stumble upon them; he seemed to know exactly where they were. This was a mystery!

Tuesday 14/07/15

Today was the first day back at school for the third term and Itsal nudged me twice in the morning while I was asleep which meant he wanted me to get out of bed right away. It was early and my alarm was due to sound thirty minutes later. I did not know why Itsal had woken me early, but I knew I needed to get out of bed to find out the reason. When I got out of bed Itsal led me by the wrist to the back door. He needed the toilet, fair enough I could understand. When Itsal came back inside he led me to Lachlan's room and as I entered it I noticed it was very warm inside the room and Lachlan had kicked his blankets off. This is what Itsal had wanted to tell me. He noticed Lachlan's room was too hot as the heater had made it warmer than it usually was. Thanks again Itsal.

Lachlan was excited to go back to school today and wanted to wait outside at the front of the house for the bus to come. For the first time this year, he agreed to wear his woollen jacket because it was so cold outside. He does not usually feel the cold weather as much as the rest of the family.

Off he went happily, into the bus and off to school. The teacher reported that Lachlan a great day and enjoyed showing the other kids photos from the holidays when he surfed and visited the train museum.

While Lachlan was at school, I had a consultation with his therapist Debbie about food issues. For just over a month now Lachlan has not wanted to eat his usual dinner which is a mix of oats, meat, fruit, vegetables and vitamins. The most prominent flavour is banana as the mix usually has two bananas in it. No one could blame him for not wanting to eat this anymore as he has been eating various versions of it since he was a baby. The problem lies with him not wanting to eat much else instead. Debbie always gives great advice about leaving foods around so that Lachlan is exposed to them and seeing others eat the foods helps as well. We ask Lachlan to handle the foods by passing them to someone or putting them into the bin as Debbie suggests. Lots of things end up in the bin at our house!

We continually work on exposing Lachlan to foods each day. We are currently working on strawberries, apples, cheese slices and sticks, sandwiches, different types of chips, different breads, and meats. These are all things he has eaten previously and Debbie said that he would be more likely to go back to these foods rather than eat completely new foods.

Lachlan has made good progress with Debbie's help and now eats a variety of different breads and drinks a healthier type of juice which contains less sugar and has no artificial additives.

Saturday 18/07/15

Lachlan will now hold and break a slice of cheese or a cheese stick. This evening he broke a slice of cheese apart and touched it on his cheek and held it to his lips while he played on the computer. I thought he was going to eat, it but instead he placed it on the floor. This was good progress for a completely new food. We had been leaving it around the house for Lachlan to become exposed to it for the past two months and I could see that he was very close to eating it! Maybe next time. Persevering will pay off eventually.

Sunday 19/07/15

Today Lachlan went on an outing with Dad. First bushwalking, and then a visit to Nanna's house.

Lachlan jumped out of the car when they arrived at the National Park for a bushwalk. He was really excited and wanted to start the walk right away. He found a path he wanted to take and once he started walking he touched some moss on the rocks and some bark which had peeled from a tree. He balanced on some logs and climbed over rocks. After he had walked for thirty minutes he came to a beach which he was very excited about. He gazed into the rock pools and liked seeing the little fish swimming around in them. Next he walked along the beach and came across some driftwood logs which he walked along. Next he dug a big hole in the sand and sat inside it.

On the way back to the car, Lachlan liked seeing the huge waves crashing onto the rocks. While he walked up the hill he stopped at times and admired the view at different levels. He liked the view of the coast which headed back to Sydney as well as watching a sea eagle which flew around in circles.

Next Lachlan went to visit his nanna Betty which was a short drive away. As soon as he arrived he approached nanna by going up close to her and then made himself at home by taking off his shoes. Next he chose one of nanna's DVDs and put it into her player and watched it. After a short visit with nanna and lunch, it was time to head back home.

In the meanwhile back at home Lachlan's other nanna visited for the day from the aged care facility nearby. When she arrived she looked at some photos on the mantelpiece, and when she saw one of Lachlan, she picked it up and kissed it. Next Mum asked where he was and whether he had moved out. Mum has dementia which made her confused and she seemed to lose track of time. She seemed relieved when I told her that Lachlan had just gone out for the day, and that he was too young to have left home. Next Mum asked where my little girl was and I told her that she had grown up and was now twenty-five years old. She then looked at her photo on the mantelpiece and nodded as she remembered Samantha had grown up.

Tuesday 21/07/15

Lachlan awoke at 3.30am this morning and I did not know the reason. Itsal came and alerted me and a few moments later Lachlan turned the light on in my room. He seemed to be in a lively mood and did not go back to sleep. When it was time to go to school he was well and truly ready for the day to start and he gladly climbed into the bus and went off to begin his day.

Wednesday 22/07/15

After school today Lachlan needed to attend a dental appointment which was a follow-up check on his recent dental work. Before he went I showed him the social story I had made so that he understood the reason for the visit. Lachlan also knew he would visit the shops afterwards to look at DVDs so he was happy with this social story which demonstrated something he was required to do, followed by something he liked to do. A happy ending.

The dentist had a few attempts to examine Lachlan's teeth, after which he was happy for this to happen. Lachlan sat up rather than lay down, as he was cautious. The dentist reported all was well with Lachlan's teeth.

While at the shops afterwards, Lachlan found a loophole as he was allowed to choose one DVD but instead chose a DVD set which contained four DVDs inside! He knew he would not have been allowed to buy four of them individually. He was very excited when he arrived home to watch his set of four DVDs.

Today at dinner time Lachlan held onto a strawberry for quite some time. We knew this was a good sign that he may start eating it. He rubbed the strawberry on his cheek at times and rolled it in his hands. Next he bought it to his mouth and touched it on his lips. As I tried to pretend I had not noticed what he was doing with the strawberry, I saw him take the tiniest bite of it. Success!

When Lachlan is interested in eating a particular food, he will want to eat that same food repeatedly, usually at the same time each day. As he has always had a limited diet, we always tried to have the very few foods he ate available to him. As a toddler he became very attached to strawberries but did not understand that there were some seasons in which strawberries didn't grow and he would become upset if there were no strawberries available at the same time each day.

Lachlan did not like the look of the strawberries to vary. He preferred them not to be too light or too red. We became strawberry experts as we found out which shops stocked strawberries and where the best ones were located. We looked all over for them, different shops in different suburbs. Looking back, I think it may have been easier to have grown the strawberries myself, but I thought it would be time consuming so didn't, and the seasons would still have changed so Lachlan would still have needed to adjust when there were no strawberries available. Eventually Lachlan became tired of eating strawberries and moved onto bananas which were much easier to obtain.

Lachlan had been reluctant to eat strawberries again after giving them up as a toddler and tonight he held onto the same strawberry for around an hour and took tiny bites of it every now and then. Any eating at all is a fantastic step in the right direction. When it became late and time for Lachlan's evening routine, he put the strawberry down and went into the kitchen and requested some bread. We told him that dinner needed to be eaten first, and then he could have some bread. He reluctantly ate a small amount of his dinner which was the usual oat mixture and contained meat, fruit, vegetables and vitamins. After this he ate some bread with jam.

Thursday 23/07/15

Lachlan was tired this morning as he often is at the end of the week due to the effect of early morning starts. Itsal nudged him several times to wake him and Lachlan eventually woke and pushed him away. When Lachlan and Itsal are not being supervised Itsal does as Lachlan asks as he understands Lachlan's nonverbal gestures. When I gave the command, Itsal jumped back onto the bed and interacted with Lachlan by nudging his face which he tried to hide underneath his pillow.

Itsal understands Lachlan's routine and his role in it and although Lachlan pushes him away at times, Itsal interacts just enough so that Lachlan does not become upset, rather, slightly inconvenienced by the nudging. Itsal found a gap uncovered by Lachlan's pyjamas which is where he nudged him with his wet nose. When this happened Lachlan turned around and gave him a pat. Lachlan was amused by his tail which wagged very fast.

After half an hour, success! Lachlan rose from his of bed and Itsal came to me for acknowledgement that he had done his job. Itsal was happy once he knew his job was done and stepped aside which allowed Lachlan to watch a DVD and get dressed for school. Itsal does not usually interact very much at this time, he just waits while the morning routine unfolds one step at a time.

Lachlan carried his bag and happily joined the others on the school bus when it arrived. He also took a small bag of toys and books to play with on the way.

Saturday 25/07/15

Today Lachlan played soccer as usual. Lachlan always seems proud of himself whenever he is asked about soccer and I think he knows other people value this. Afterwards he went to the park and choose between two versions of a song to be sung by Dad by pointing to one hand or another when asked this one or that one? Lachlan also rode his adult size trike which he enjoyed greatly.

Tuesday 28/07/15

This morning the routine went very well. The school bus arrived early and we noticed there was a different worker inside the bus. Lachlan was slightly disturbed when he saw the new person, but I reassured him and he climbed into the bus as usual. Lachlan held one of his favourite toys, a long yellow wand which played a song in a Chinese language. None of us know what the words of the song mean. Lachlan likes the music and singing it produces.

While Lachlan was at school, I had a consultation with his dietician who in the past had given us some excellent tips and advice for Lachlan. We discussed Lachlan's current vitamin supplements as well as the results of a recent blood test which showed Lachlan's iron to be low, but within the normal range. The test also showed slightly low bicarbonate, calcium and albumin.

The dietician told me about an iron supplement, small sachets of water which contained iron that I could add to Lachlan's usual juice which he wouldn't be able to taste. Lachlan also needed more protein which I could add in very small amounts only, lest he taste it and reject his dinner altogether. I need to be careful! The dietician also gave me some great ideas such as grinding nuts into a powder and adding them to Lachlan's dinner. She recommended grated goats' cheese be added to Lachlan's dinner as an extra calcium source. What a helpful person!

Friday 31/07/15

Today was a pupil free day so no school for Lachlan and he asked to go shopping. After I agreed to take him shopping, I explained that we also needed to go and pay a bill as well as buy some groceries. Lachlan nodded in agreement. Now that he knows he is going shopping, when I asked him to get dressed he could not do it fast enough. Often it takes more than one attempt, but today Lachlan was clearly ready to go out.

When we arrived at the shops he pointed in the direction he wanted us to go. He led me to a children's ride and was excited when a little girl ran over and jumped up on the ride and seemed to be as excited about it as he was. Lachlan always seems so happy to see other children enjoying themselves.

Next we visited Lachlan's favourite DVD shop where he looked at the collection of children's DVDs as well as others. It seemed as though he was looking for something in particular but I did not know what he was looking for. The shop assistant asked us if he could help find something as he could see Lachlan was searching for a DVD. I told the shop assistant that Lachlan was just browsing and all of a sudden Lachlan chose five DVDs and handed them to me. I told him to choose one only so he picked the first one he found. I guess he thought it was worth a try.

Next I reminded Lachlan that we needed to pay a bill and went downstairs in order to do it. Lachlan was reluctant to continue going down the floors, but I reminded him that it was important, so he followed me down the floors. When we arrived I knew the reason for his reluctance. There was once a children's ride on the same floor which Lachlan had been frightened of and this was one of the reasons he would not go to shopping centres. Now Lachlan listened to me when I told him there was nothing to worry about when he passed by the ride and held Itsal's harness.

While doing the grocery shopping we ran into a friend of mine who Lachlan had met just once before. Lachlan seemed to remember her as he waved to her and he waited patiently while we chatted. He found some bread rolls he liked in a cabinet in the bakery and placed two of them into a bag and we went to the self-service counter which Lachlan used like an expert.

I placed various items on the counter and he selected the appropriate pictures and the amount we had of each item. Then he put the items in bags. He will now touch some vegetables while shopping as he knows there are no expectations for him to eat them. Knowing how to use the self-serve counter is a very useful skill for him to have.

Back at home, we baked some cakes. While Lachlan had never really been interested in cooking, he seemed to take more interest in it lately. In the past he had found cooking rather revolting and would cringe when he saw ingredients being combined. With Debbie's help we have been able to desensitise Lachlan to many foods. Fantastic. Thanks Debbie!

Lachlan cracked an egg and put it into the mixing bowl being careful not to get any of the egg on his hands. He tipped in the milk and enjoyed mixing it with a wooden spoon. He placed blue paper cases into the baking tray, but ran off when he saw how we needed to put the cake mix into the little cases with two spoons. He liked icing them with yellow icing and he stuck on little edible stickers. When the cakes were finished Lachlan held one near his face while he played on the computer. He did not eat it but it was step in the right direction. Maybe next time!

This afternoon we went to one of Lachlan's favourite parks. He had a turn on the swing and asked me to push him, by pushing his feet. He realised he could go much higher this way than he could by swinging himself. Lachlan does not like to not hold onto the swing which often unnerves onlookers, but he has excellent sense of balance and has never fallen off.

Lachlan played on the equipment and there was a slide and some pipes to climb down. There were stairs which Lachlan likes to jump off. Once he jumped from the very top one and hurt himself, so I told him to jump from the bottom two only, which he did.

Some other children played in a rope tunnel and Lachlan wanted to join in and climb with them. There was a mother and her two children who asked how I was and told me that she was trying to use up some of the children's energy before the sun went down, to which I replied, "Same with us". Her daughter who looked around three years of age played inside the rope tunnel. Lachlan, being tall for his age, looked like a giant in comparison.

Lachlan could hardly wait to play inside the tunnel, but I asked him to wait as I worried there would not be enough room inside the tunnel for the little girl and him together, and I did not want her to get squashed. He waited until the tiny girl came out from the other side of the tunnel. A little boy sat near the entrance of the tunnel as well. He did not seem interested in going inside so Lachlan moved past him to enter the tunnel. Lachlan made his usual vocalisations (which those who know him hardly notice anymore). The boy asked his mother, "What's he doing?" And his mum replied, "He just wants to play, the same as you do," and the boy did not ask any further questions. If only all parents responded in the same way as this mother.

Next, Lachlan waited for the little girl to finish on the rocking bridge before he had his turn. While he waited, a little boy (the girl's brother who was around 5 years old) watched on. The boy asked his mum, who was busy with a baby, "Why doesn't he say please and ask if he can get on the bridge?" His mother replied, "Maybe he doesn't have the right words, but look how good he is at balancing on the bridge." What a perfect response from this mum I thought, to have pointed out the similarities and not the differences. Lachlan hears the comments people make about him in public and few are as positive as this.

Next we went for a walk on the walking track at the park and when we got to the end of the track Lachlan signed "More" and showed me on his fingers that he wanted to walk the track three times.

We started off walking and then Lachlan ran fast, really fast and luckily I had the right shoes on so I could keep up with him. He did not get tired. We combined jogging and walking three times on the track which added up to over five kilometres.

This evening at Lachlan's bath time, I added some Epsom salts mixed with Bi-carb soda recommended by the dietician. Shortly afterwards Lachlan had dinner, took a turn on the trampoline, and listened to music in his room. He wanted to be by himself and signed "Finished" when I checked on him.

When it was time for bed, I held Lachlan's hand as usual and he fell asleep in less than five minutes which I could not believe as sometimes it takes Lachlan an hour or more to fall asleep. He was so relaxed and happy.

Must have been those bath salts. He had an excellent sleep overnight.

Chapter 8
August 2015

Saturday 01/08/15

Lachlan played soccer as usual for Saturday mornings. This is the third year he has played and each year he enjoys it more than the one before. When he first started he found it overwhelming being on a field with a large crowd of people all in one place. He was also unsure about doing many of the ball tricks, however, he liked the idea of being part of a soccer team so we persevered. This morning he practiced kicking the ball into the net and waited patiently for his turn each time.

In the afternoon Lachlan went to the aquatic centre and leapt out of the car when he arrived as he was very excited to be there. He sung to himself on the way in. Once inside there were some teenagers competing in one of the pools and Lachlan sat and watched them for a while. First of all Lachlan ran through the water and then had a turn on a slide. Next he saw a giant slide which he wanted to have a turn on but as the pool would not allow two people on it at a time, we thought it best to say no to

Lachlan's request as he sometimes does not see the need to follow the rules. We thought he may stop half way in the slide and not want to come out as he has done before. Lachlan did not seem to mind, he just kept on playing in the water.

He floated on his back for some time and propelled himself along rather fast in all directions. Even though there were various people with tattoos at the pool today which Lachlan pointed out, he did not try to touch their tattoos like he usually did.

This reminded me of a day at the aquatic centre when we had been swimming and Lachlan had spotted a man in the distance with a large tattoo which he wanted to have a closer look at. I had not realised where he was headed at the time and thought he had spotted a pool toy which another child played with and wanted to take a closer look. A second possibility was that Lachlan wanted to enter the whirlpool which he loved. When he started to head off in another direction I followed him not knowing tattoos were on his mind. Half way across the pool he spotted the man whose tattoo he was interested in and before I could stop him he grabbed the man's arm and cuddled into it. The man just smiled and said, "he's OK" and I felt relieved that he had not been upset by Lachlan's response. Sometimes there is just not enough time to stop Lachlan from doing these sorts of things!

Another time while grocery shopping, in front of us at the checkout, there was a man loading his groceries onto the counter. Lachlan pointed and stood up in the trolley and I knew this meant he wanted to get out of the trolley. As he had been known to run off, I encouraged him to stand in between the man in front of us and myself. Lachlan seemed happy and then I noticed the man had a large tattoo on his arm. All of a sudden while I loaded the groceries onto the counter, Lachlan grabbed the man's tattooed arm and cuddled into it. The man started to laugh loudly (thankfully), and I told him that Lachlan loved tattoos. He replied, "Don't get them, little man, they are very addictive". I was unsure if Lachlan understood what that meant but he was very happy the man with the big arm tattoo was talking to him.

Today Lachlan was too busy playing in the water to worry about tattoos. He swam around and around in the whirlpool going as fast as he could. After three-and-a half hours Lachlan looked a little tired so we did a five minute apart, which reminded Lachlan that soon it would be time to go home. First there were three more turns at playing in the pool, then two, then the last turn because Lachlan does not like it when things suddenly stop. After the countdown Lachlan accepted that is was time to leave. He was also tired after swimming for the afternoon.

Monday 03/08/15

This morning Itsal woke me at 3.00 a.m. and I heard that Lachlan was awake. He was in a very lively mood and as it seemed colder than usual in his room I suggested he wear an extra pyjama top, which he did. I sat and held his hand and hoped he would go back to sleep. Half an hour later he was still awake and I had an idea. Knowing that Lachlan sometimes does not go back to sleep when he wakes early, I used his beanbag as a bed on the floor to avoid sitting for a long period of time and I covered myself with a blanket. I was still able to hold Lachlan's hand and at around 5.30 a.m. both of us fell asleep. When my alarm sounded it did not wake Lachlan and I was very pleased he had gone back to sleep so that he would be less tired throughout the school day.

When it is was time to wake Lachlan, Itsal nudged him a few times and he woke up. He was in a very happy mood and wanted to get out of bed straight away. He happily joined the school bus and went off to school.

When he returned from school he played in the back room and I heard some rustling in there. When I went in I noticed Lachlan had pulled the Christmas tree out of the cupboard and he gestured for me to put it up in the lounge room. I showed him the calendar and reminded him that Christmas was in December so there was still a few months to wait. Maybe he thought it was about time for some new toys. Lachlan like many children, loves Christmas time.

Tuesday 04/08/15

This evening we were very pleased as Lachlan took a small bite of a strawberry which he'd been holding onto for half an hour. Each night he is given either a piece of cheese or a cheese stick along with an apple or some strawberries. After this he has his dinner but often eats very little of it. Hopefully he will start to eat the cheese soon as he now is at the stage of breaking it up and placing it near his mouth. He held onto it for thirty minutes as this is how he gets used to foods.

Lachlan has done this for the last month and it seems as if he is very close to eating the cheese. He has a slight calcium deficiency so that would be fantastic. We cannot force him eat foods he does not want but hope he will change his mind soon.

Thursday 06/08/15

Each morning this week Lachlan has taken a heated wheat bag with him on the school bus. He did not mind that it was bright pink and heart shaped. He was not concerned about the opinions of other passengers on the bus. Lachlan has been in very a happy mood all week and I wondered if the new vitamin supplements he had started taking had made a difference.

This evening while Lachlan jumped on the trampoline, we saw and heard fireworks. Lachlan enjoyed the display and when they finished he signed the "More" sign. Funny that Lachlan thought we could somehow extend the firework display he had enjoyed so much.

Saturday 08/08/15

This morning Lachlan woke up and played with Itsal and also on the computer. He stood near the heater which usually makes other people nervous, his grandmother in particular. I am confident he would not continue to stand near the heater once he felt his clothes become warm as I have seen many times that he moves away, the same as most other people.

Next Lachlan played songs backwards which he found on YouTube. He also played songs in different languages some which were unfamiliar to me.

At soccer this morning, Lachlan practised the skill of stopping and turning the ball with his foot many times and stayed engaged until the session ended.

Sunday 09/08/15

Lachlan went on an outing to ride miniature electric trains on a track which ran through bushland. The train consisted of three carriages which held around thirty people. Lachlan was first reluctant to join the train ride as the area was crowded with people but eventually decided to ride the train and ended up having four rides in total.

After the train ride Lachlan visited a farm which had a playground attached. There were three old farm houses there and at one of them there was a water pump which Lachlan found and played with. Next he played in the playground on the slide and swings.

At dinner time, Lachlan broke up the pieces of cheese we had given him and put them near his lips but did not eat them. He seemed very close to eating them so each night we continue to offer him either cheese slices or sticks. Sometimes he gestures for me to eat them and I pretend to enjoy them and make it seem like a positive experience hoping Lachlan will want to follow my lead.

This evening Lachlan wanted me to eat the cheese stick. He brought it to me and gestured for me to place it in my mouth, which I did, but I planned to remove it when Lachlan was not watching. Lachlan watched intently to see exactly where the cheese stick went, so I had to eat it and almost vomited! Lachlan seemed slightly happy and amused!

After the cheese stick experience I made cheese on toast and left it on a plate near Lachlan so that it would be within his view and maybe he would consider eating it. I left Lachlan in the lounge room for a while and when I went back I noticed that he had eaten some of the cheese on toast! This was a big deal as it is a goal we had been working on for some time! This was very exciting!

I told Lachlan I was proud of him for trying something new and he replied, "Are you?" It was like a miracle when he spoke as it is so rare. Whenever Lachlan speaks we always wonder what it was about the present time that prompted him to speak.

Tuesday 11/08/15

Today there was another session with Debbie, Lachlan's therapist who is working with him on the food issues. Debbie was pleased when I told her of Lachlan's progress with the cheese toast and the strawberry and we agreed on a plan for the month ahead. We planned to set Lachlan up for success by offering him a small amount of his usual dinner every second night until he begins to eat other foods which we would offer on alternate nights. We need to make some very small changes by offering him foods only slightly different from foods he currently eats, has shown interest in or has eaten in the past. Then we branch out from those.

Debbie suggested we keep trying toast with cheese which may head towards him eventually eating a cheese pizza. Another idea suggested was to try smooth battered chicken nuggets instead of crumbed ones. Debbie also suggested varying the jams he eats as well as the types of bread rolls.

Each day we offer Lachlan cheese and fruit. Sometimes we offer bacon and Lachlan touches it. Lachlan ate bacon as a toddler and I think he remembered it. Maybe he will start eating it again as he seemed rather interested in it.

During the night I heard Lachlan vocalising and knew he had woken. It was unusual that Itsal had not come to wake me to let me know, I thought. When I checked on Lachlan, I felt his forehead and found it was burning with fever and I noticed that Itsal sat right next to his bed and not on it as he usually did. Itsal seemed to know that Lachlan was sick and did not want to leave him to come and tell me that Lachlan was awake as he normally would. Maybe Itsal also knew that if he slept on Lachlan's bed it would make Lachlan even hotter. Clever boy Itsal!

Wednesday 12/08/15

Lachlan did not go to school today as he was sick. He was sleepy throughout the day and did not eat anything the entire day. He did have some drinks as least. Itsal sat next to Lachlan for the day while he watched television and slept on and off.

Thursday 13/08/15

Lachlan was unwell at home. In the evening the doctor visited him which he was prepared for, as I had made a social story on his iPad so that Lachlan would know what to expect. He complied with the examination while the doctor listened to his chest and examined his ears and throat. Lachlan was at first reluctant to have his temperature taken with an unfamiliar type of thermometer so I had a turn first and next he had his turn. The doctor told us Lachlan has a virus and did not prescribe any medication for him.

Lachlan's attitude towards being examined has changed a lot as when he was younger he would not have allowed an examination like he had today. He is more at ease now and understands the doctor is trying to help him get well.

Again, Lachlan did not eat all day. The doctor told us this was fine and that when his fever subsided he should start eating again.

Friday 14/08/15

Lachlan was still sick and sleepy during the day. He watched television and when I returned from the kitchen to check on him he had fallen asleep while he held his iPad. The iPad showed a picture of him asleep on the lounge that I had taken once before when he was unwell and had fallen asleep while he sat up. It seemed he found that photo because he was tired and wanted to sleep on the lounge like he did in the photo. He would easily remember each and every photo in the iPad as Lachlan remembers things like that.

Lachlan was still sick but managed to eat some bread rolls, so I guessed he must have been a little less sick than yesterday. During the night Itsal woke me as Lachlan coughed a great deal. Eventually Lachlan and Itsal both went back to sleep.

15/08/15-17/08/15

Lachlan was still sick but slowly getting better. He gradually ate more and slept less each day.

Tuesday 18/08/15

Lachlan visited the doctor and was happy enough to be examined. The doctor explained each step of the examination to Lachlan and took it slowly which Lachlan liked, as he knew what to expect. The doctor prescribed some antibiotics for Lachlan's cough as it seemed to have gotten worse. We wondered if Lachlan would be willing to take the antibiotics and we raised this concern to the doctor. He and his wife kindly offered to come to our house to assist Lachlan. We were grateful but declined the offer as we wanted to give the medicine to Lachlan with his usual juice and thought he would accept it this way. The medicine was raspberry flavoured and Lachlan needed only a very small dose which was mixed in his juice and he accepted it. We were very grateful the doctor had found a medicine which had a taste Lachlan accepted and that now he was able to recover faster.

Wednesday 19/08/15

Lachlan has all three doses of his medication and did not wake during the night. He was recovering.

Thursday 20/08/15, Friday 21/08/15

Lachlan stayed home from school these two days and planned to go back to school on Monday.

Sunday 23/08/15

Lachlan requested a trip to the park using a PECS picture. He directed Dad to a park quite a long way from home that he had been to only once before. Lachlan led the way which was a different route than he had travelled last time. We were unsure how he knew which streets led to the park so far away from home, but somehow he did.

Monday 24/08/15

Back to school today. I think Lachlan had missed his friends but found it a little difficult to wake up early and go back to the school routine after being home so long. Itsal knew exactly what to do and nudged Lachlan until he sat up in bed and then reminded me to take the DVD player out into the next room. Itsal did this by touching the DVD player as he looked at me, as he knew moving the DVD player was the next part of the school routine.

Lachlan happily watched DVDs once out of bed and by the time the school bus came he was well and truly ready to go.

Tuesday 25/08/15

This afternoon Lachlan watched classical music, Mozart. Lachlan went as close as he could to the television set and inspected the musical instruments. He was especially interested in the violins and I wondered if he had a violin whether he would be interested in learning how to play. A good future Christmas present perhaps. Lachlan has been interested in musical instruments for some time now.

Wednesday 26/08/15

This morning Lachlan was reluctant to get out of bed. Itsal helped by nudging him which made Lachlan sit up. Lachlan signed the "Finished" sign to Itsal as he wanted to be left alone. Itsal seemed to understand Lachlan's request and I was unsure if Itsal saw the hand sign

Lachlan made or whether he just knew by the vocalisations Lachlan made. Itsal jumped off the bed and observed for further instructions. After a little while I played a DVD in Spanish as I think Spanish is Lachlan's favourite language and when Lachlan heard it, he leapt out of bed to get ready for school.

This afternoon Lachlan visited a shopping centre which was close by and one he had visited once before. He enjoyed the rides there and rode on all three of them. This evening Lachlan ate a small amount of his dinner and held onto a huge strawberry for thirty minutes before he took a few small bites of it and put it aside which was still good progress.

After dinner Lachlan had a turn on the outdoor trampoline as he usually does unless it's raining. It had rained this afternoon and even after the trampoline was dried Lachlan's clothes became damp. When he came back inside I suggested to him that he change his damp clothes. As I was about to assist him to change his clothes Lachlan said "Why?" Which was first time Lachlan had ever said the word "Why". How exciting! It is always wonderful to hear Lachlan say even one word. Any word. We would be happy to hear even a swear word!

Next Lachlan listened to music and danced around in his room while a CD played various songs, most of which he liked. He operates the CD player much better than anyone else is able to and of course he remembers the order and number of the songs on every CD. He scrolls through the numbers to find the song he wants and then plays it. He played a song about a crocodile and I could not believe it when he said "Croc" clearly once, and then said it three more times. I wondered what the reason was that Lachlan said two new words today, but there was nothing different about today – the routine had been the same as usual.

While Lachlan listened to the music he came to sit on my lap and tried to bump his head on mine as he likes the sensation of pressure on his head. I knocked on his forehead gently with my fist and he smiled and signed the "More" sign. He seemed to enjoy it and asked several times for "More". Lachlan also enjoys the sensation of someone pulling his hair, he does not seem to find it painful as he laughs and keeps asking for "More". I told Lachlan that I did not like it if someone pulled my hair and he answered by signing "More" because he did like it.

Thursday 27/08/2015

After looking at Lachlan's costume options for dress-up day for book week tomorrow, I found the costumes all looked too small. Thinking that Lachlan might have been unhappy in a tight outfit, we asked him if he wanted to wear some football clothes to school. He seemed happy about that as he loves to wear the football jersey Uncle Jim gave him.

This afternoon Lachlan played fetch outside with Itsal. Itsal was very excited and ran around and around in circles as fast as he could. It didn't seem like he would run into anyone even though he ran so fast it looked like it would have been hard to stop. Itsal's movements were very precise and we were surprised to see a large dog with so much control. Thanks Righteous Pups Australia. He is perfect!

This evening Lachlan took a bite of a cheese stick. How exciting and we hoped he would keep it up. Persistence has paid off.

Friday 28/08/15

Today was dress-up day for book week. Once Lachlan had his football clothes on, he was eager to go to school. We waited outside in the driveway for the school bus to come and in the meantime Lachlan watched a huge truck as it arrived for work at the building site next door to our house. The bus arrived a few moments later and Lachlan took his little heat pack with him and stepped onto the bus.

When Lachlan arrived home from school he was very excited. He loves Fridays. After being asked what he wanted to do this afternoon he typed on his iPad "I want to go to the park". While in the car Lachlan pointed and showed the way to the park he wanted to visit. He knows the way to all the parks. He chose a local park which he had been to once before and once there he walked along a bridge which overlooked lots of streets and another park. He pointed in the direction of the park he saw, to let us know he wanted to visit. He knew all the streets and which way to go to get there. Once he arrived he played in the giant sand pit which must have been the reason he chose this particular park.

This afternoon we heard some very exciting news being that Lachlan's project has been approved and funded by My Choice Matters. One of his goals is to learn to surf and he will be using a surf simulator at a local centre each week to achieve this. Lachlan will have one on one lessons each week with an instructor. The next part of the goal is that he will join a junior surfing group and surf at the beach. He will be able to make new friends with other children who share the same interest as him and when I told l him this news and he was very excited. Surfing is Lachlan's most favourite pastime, as well as swimming.

This evening Lachlan could not stop laughing as I told him a story about how I would become sick and vomit when I was a child if rode on any rides which spun around. I told him about the things I had eaten before the rides (which for some reason I still remembered in detail) and I explained the movement of the rides. Lachlan seems to be the opposite and absolutely loves spinning around and rides do not make him feel sick at all.

Lachlan kept on signing "More" and laughed continuously as he wanted to hear more about the ride story and when he stopped, ALL OF A SUDDEN AND FOR THE FIRST TIME EVER HE SAID, "I LOVE YOU." WOW! Even though I heard it, it was hard to believe. This was amazing! After a while I told him, "I love ..." and then paused and Lachlan replied, "Me"!

It seemed that all the laughing had made Lachlan tired and he fell asleep in a few minutes without having needed to hold my hand. When I left the room, Itsal climbed onto Lachlan's bed for the night.

Saturday 29/08/15

This morning Lachlan played a computer game and chose the correct answers in Japanese!

Next Lachlan attended a gala day at soccer. Today soccer was played differently due to the gala day and there were a few short games. Lachlan stayed and participated for a while but did not want to stay for the whole day. Once he left he visited the usual set of shops which he often visits after soccer.

He had a turn on his favourite ride and afterwards inspected it from many different angles inside the shopping centre. He went to one end of the shopping centre and looked back at the ride and watched the lights on top of it and observed the difference from the new angle. He walked up some stairs and watched the ride from the top and then watched it from the bottom stairs. He liked seeing lights reflected from shiny surfaces around the ride and he looked at a mirror on a stand which sold sunglasses and a black highly polished sign in front of a shop to observe how the light from the ride lit up the surfaces.

Sunday 30/08/15

This morning we went to church. We were slightly late (which was usual for us) and we could not sneak in without being noticed, for two reasons. The first reason was that no seats were available in the back row so we needed to sit in a row which was only three quarters of the way back, which meant more people could see us. The other reason was that Lachlan was quite excited to be there and was making happy vocalisations. He sat for almost the entire church service, being the longest he has ever sat in church. Lachlan ate bread rolls during the church service and patted and hugged Itsal at times who lay at his feet.

Someone needs to invent a miniature vacuum cleaner small enough to fit in my handbag so that I would be able to pick up the trail of bread crumbs that usually follow Lachlan.

It was hard to believe how much Lachlan had changed, by having Itsal in church. When everyone stood to sing, Lachlan took the opportunity to race up onto the stage with the singers and the band (which nobody seemed disturbed about), and some could definitely see the funny side of it.

Sometimes Lachlan plays the instruments when the band has finished, and Jean plays a song on the piano for him. Maybe this was what Lachlan was after today. Later on when Jean and I chatted she had said she thought it was "beautiful" that Lachlan wanted to join in. Lachlan is accepted and appreciated here, and of course Itsal is always very popular. It was a pleasant sunny day, so Lachlan played outside in the grounds with some other children from church.

This afternoon Lachlan went to a local Greek festival. There were a lot of people there and Lachlan was very excited when he saw the dodgem cars and asked to have a turn. When Lachlan drove the dodgem car, he smashed into as many people and attendants as possible. He laughed and laughed as he smashed into the other cars. Lachlan tried to find the biggest looking man or boy and smash into their car. One of the boys chased Lachlan in his car for a while but got bumped out of the way.

Next Lachlan went on the jumping castle and after a while we noticed we could not see him anymore. We asked the attendant whether it was possible for Lachlan to have exited the ride without anyone noticing, but he said there wasn't, and then we saw Lachlan had been hiding behind one of the pillars on the castle. With every jump he bounced as high as he could and was very tired when he finished.

This evening I left the fridge door open while I reached for a kitchen utensil and I noticed Itsal closed it by pushing it with his snout. I left the door open once more to see what Itsal would do and again he closed the door with his snout. Clever boy!

Monday 31/08/15

This morning Lachlan was tired and found it hard waking up early to go to school. Lachlan and Itsal have worked out their own language and Itsal seemed to understand what Lachlan wanted. When I tried to wake Lachlan, he placed his pillow over his head and signed the "Finished" sign. If Itsal did not know the sign then he must have known what Lachlan's vocalisations meant as when Lachlan signed the "Finished" sign Itsal jumped down from his bed. After a short while I gave Itsal a command to get back onto the bed and he sat on Lachlan's pillow which stopped Lachlan from lying down. Lachlan and Itsal played and then Lachlan got out of bed, when he was ready.

When the school bus arrived home this afternoon, Lachlan did not jump out as usual. When the door opened I saw that he had gone to sleep on Emma's lap.

He was in a quiet mood during the afternoon and did not want to go out today. Too tired perhaps.

After dinner when we played in Lachlan's room, he said "Oh wow!" and also "Gail." Mum would have been better, but I was happy to hear him say a new word. It was fantastic that he had spoken some new words recently. His family always wants to know his thoughts.

Lately, I've noticed that Lachlan will answer questions when asked by nodding yes, or shaking his head to indicate, no. He indicates no more often and if he is unsure, he answers no just in case.

Chapter 9
September 2015

Wednesday 02/09/15

This afternoon Leah from the swim centre contacted us to let us know she had found a suitable instructor for Lachlan's surfing lessons and soon Lachlan would be able to begin his lessons as part of his My Choice Matters project. Lachlan was very excited when I told him this wonderful news and he went to his iPad and found a video of the surf simulator and watched it to remind himself how much fun was in store.

This evening Lachlan was served some cheese as part of his plan with therapist, Debbie. He broke the cheese into little pieces and placed a small piece on his lips. One of these days he will eat it! Itsal sat alongside Lachlan and I wondered if it would help if Lachlan saw Itsal eat some cheese first. I gave Itsal a piece of cheese as Lachlan watched intently. Itsal ate the cheese as instructed but seemed slightly surprised as this was outside of his usual feeding routine.

Lachlan had a bath to which we added a mix of Epsom salts and Bi-carb soda to help him relax which worked like a charm as at bedtime Lachlan fell asleep in under ten minutes.

Thursday 03/09/15

This evening Lachlan did his homework and as we read a bedtime story he covered his head with a pillow. Lachlan was tired as he often is late in the week. When I started to talk about surfing he was interested so removed the pillow from his head. I told him that he would start surfing lessons soon and that Leah from the swim centre had been working hard to organise them for him. Lachlan said her name and I knew that he remembered her and the surf simulator. He was so excited about starting the lessons and even answered, "I do," when I asked him about them.

Every now and then Lachlan says, "I do," and I think it's one way that he shows he wants to be independent. Often he will say it when he prefers to do something for himself such as brush his teeth, his hair or open a gift.

Recently, Lachlan has been talking every day, at least once a day. We wonder whether this will increase.

Friday 04/09/15

This morning as soon as Lachlan saw me, he signed "Finished", so I told him, "Three more," which meant he could "Finish" me three more times and then it would be time to get out of bed. Five minutes later I returned to his room with Itsal and Lachlan again signed "Finished" directed at me and then directed at Itsal. Itsal understood his request and leapt off the bed. Next I told him, "Two more," and I left him alone for a few minutes. When I returned to his room, he jumped up out of bed and was ready to begin the day. That was easier than I thought!

Itsal approached me for a pat which confirmed to him that his job was finished for now, and Lachlan sat on the lounge and watched DVDs until the school bus arrived. When I told him the bus had come, he laid down on the lounge, in protest, which I thought was more about being a nine-year-old than it was about having a disability.

I reminded Lachlan that his friends were on the bus and waiting for him, and that it was Friday and soon the weekend would be here. After that he reluctantly walked in the direction of the bus, but held onto my arm.

When Lachlan returned from school, he had a big brown bag which he pointed to as he wanted me to look inside. There were some Father's Day presents he had made at school. He showed me a gingerbread man which he made and pointed to, and told me "Go" which meant he wanted me to open it. After I opened it he felt the hard gingerbread surface. I wondered if he would eat it, but knew it would have been unlikely as it usually takes a number of months of exposure to a new food before Lachlan tries it. He did not eat it, but was interested in it because he had made it, and that was a good start.

Lachlan played a game on the computer which required the player to type in a number which appeared on the screen which was a pretend mobile number. Lachlan could have completed this easily but chose to do it backwards so he entered the correct digits in last to make the game last longer. He often does this as he knows that once he types the correct number in, the screen will change and that part of the game will over.

Next it was bath time which Lachlan wanted finished as soon as possible as he wanted to get back to the computer game he was enjoying so much. He signed "Finished" a few times and I knew he was in a hurry for his bath to end. He had a quick wash and finished his bath and while he was getting dressed he pointed to the bathroom door and spoke, "Out there," which was the first time ever he had ever spoken those words. It was very exciting!

Lachlan's family feel sure that Itsal will continue to have a very positive impact. Lachlan speaks more and is much calmer since Itsal came to live with us. It has been seventeen months now and Lachlan is a completely changed boy. He has the confidence to go just about anywhere now, even without Itsal. The change we have seen already is really quite incredible.

Lachlan woke during the night which there did not appear to be a reason for. Neither Lachlan nor Itsal seemed concerned about anything, which was perhaps the reason Itsal had not woken me. After I checked on Lachlan I rested on the bean bag which I placed next to his bed and eventually Lachlan and I both fell asleep.

Saturday 05/09/15

Lachlan went to a local school fair this morning where he drove a dodgem car, jumped on a jumping castle and bought a DVD he found there.

This evening Lachlan broke some cheese slices apart but did not eat them. He held onto them for a while and touched his face and lips with them at times. It seemed so close that he would eat them, but not this time. Maybe one on these days. I also made some toast with cheese and left it around for him to see and I made his usual oat mixture which he did not want to eat very much of tonight.

Lachlan noticed the cheese toast and every now and then he looked over at it and eventually decided to touch it. When I offered it to him, he accepted it and held onto it. Knowing it was best to leave him alone with this, I stayed in the kitchen. When I checked fifteen minutes later, I noticed that two pieces of the toast had gone and just a few small pieces of crust remained. Success at last!

This was what we had hoped for months now. Persevering had paid off. Debbie, you are a genius!

After the Epsom salt and Bicarb bath Lachlan fell asleep without holding my hand and he slept all night without waking.

Sunday 06/09/15

Lachlan went to another fair and was very enthusiastic when he saw pony rides were available. Lachlan looked at the ponies from a distance and moved closer and closer toward them. He looked at each one of them and was particularly interested in a charcoal coloured pony and when it was free Lachlan moved closer to have a ride on it. When he sat on the pony he pulled the mane gently and laid his head on it and gave the pony a big hug, which amused some onlookers. Lachlan also went on a carousel horse ride but he liked the charcoal pony much better.

This evening while Lachlan had his bath, I was busy cooking dinner. Thinking that the dinner would be safe to leave for a few moments, I went into the lounge room and became interested in a television segment. After a couple of minutes Itsal came in to the lounge room and looked at me letting me know he wanted something. Part of me wondered why he couldn't have waited a few more minutes but he seemed unusually agitated and I knew he needed something immediately. He refused to sit – he stood and waited for me until I followed him. He seemed so relieved when I agreed to follow him to see what he wanted.

As I entered the kitchen I saw that it was filled with smoke. So much for the smoke alarms! The water had boiled dry and some very brown meat sat in the fry pan. What an amazing dog! I opened the door to let some of the smoke escape and Itsal seized my wrist and put it in his mouth. He took me to the back door as he was unhappy about me being in a smoke-filled kitchen and he did this four times until I reassured him it was alright to stay in the kitchen. As the smoke disappeared through the door, Itsal became more settled. Once the danger had passed he became calm again and I wondered how Itsal would have reacted if Lachlan had been in another room and not safe in the bathroom.

There was another time when Itsal had been extremely helpful, although everyday Itsal helps keep Lachlan in a calm happy mood. I remembered a time when Itsal had only been with us a few weeks and that afternoon, we went to Linda's house where we had been invited for afternoon tea to introduce Itsal to our friends Linda, and Team L.

Itsal was a big hit with everyone and it was a lovely afternoon. When we returned from Linda's house it was dark, around 7 p.m. and when Samantha checked on her little dog Honey, she was nowhere to be found. Samantha became distressed when she could not find Honey and we all tried looking for her, and considered the next step. Knowing our backyard was fully enclosed we could not understand how Honey could have left the back yard. Samantha scanned the backyard for some time, and called out to Honey but there was no response. The only conclusion we could come to was that Honey must have dug underneath the fence, which would have been the only way she could have got out. It was too dark to clearly see if there were any new holes in the yard. We would have to wait until morning.

Then we had an idea to ask Itsal to track Honey. We remembered from the training at Righteous Pups Australia that Itsal had been trained to track. It was also great fun practicing tracking during our handler training. We knew Itsal was trained to track Lachlan but we were unsure whether Itsal could track another dog, but we thought it was worth a try. We hoped Itsal would pinpoint the place in the yard where Honey had escaped and we could try and find her from there. I placed Itsal in his tracking harness and showed him Honey's blanket and gave him the command to start tracking.

Samantha held Itsal's harness and he pulled her towards various areas of the fence and then became fixed on a particular area and would not move. Itsal kept going in and out of the bushes in a specific location until Samantha heard something rustling in the bushes. We shone the torch in the bushes and tried to see what caused the noise, and finally Honey crawled out from undergrowth. Honey seemed sick and shaky and could barely walk and we did not know what had happened to her. Samantha checked Honey and phoned the vet who thought Honey may have eaten something which was poisonous. Samantha monitored her overnight and was ready to take her to the emergency vet rooms should her condition have deteriorated further. The next day Honey seemed much better, almost back to her usual self. We would have never found her without Itsal's help as she had been too sick to move. Thank you Itsal!

Back at home this evening the doctor came to visit Lachlan as he had puffy watery eyes and a deep cough. There had not been time to prepare a social story so I just told Lachlan that the doctor would visit him.

When the doctor arrived he was greeted with a big hug from Lachlan. The doctor examined Lachlan's chest and ears and then gave me the thermometer to have a turn first, and next Lachlan had his turn. The doctor asked if Lachlan would allow his throat to be examined and I explained that he would allow it if the tongue depressor was not used. Lachlan opened his mouth fully three times and long enough for the examination which made it the most successful examination ever! The doctor suggested Lachlan stay home from school tomorrow so that I could keep an eye on him.

Monday 07/09/15

Lachlan was happy when he awoke by himself (instead of being woken by myself or Itsal) as he knew this meant it was not a school day. Lachlan likes school and is usually happy to attend but he also likes staying home especially when he is not feeling his usual self. He coughed at times and he and Itsal sat right in front of the heater. Itsal is watchful and usually sits in front of Lachlan which prevents Lachlan from becoming too close to the heater.

Lachlan watched YouTube videos in different languages and played matching games on the computer. He played with Itsal and rode him as he would a horse. Itsal did not seem to mind at all, he seemed to enjoy the attention Lachlan gave him. Sometimes Itsal becomes tired of playing and will head to the back room for a sleep, but not today. Lachlan and Itsal played all day.

Tuesday 08/09/15

Itsal woke me at 3.45 a.m. as he nudged my arm, and I could hear that Lachlan had woken. I checked on him, but there did not seem to be any reason for him to have woken up so early. Lachlan played with a toy while in bed so I went back to bed and shortly after Lachlan fell asleep and woke up again at 5.45 a.m.

Lachlan stayed awake which gave him extra time to get ready for school but instead of heading to the bathroom to get dressed for school he decided to sit near the heater and watch the television instead. When it was time for Lachlan to dress in his school uniform he was reluctant and shook his head in disapproval. He did this three times and then Itsal assisted as he already understood the situation and knew what needed to be achieved. Itsal went over to Lachlan and gently nudged him near his face. He also tried to lick his Lachlan's face which prompted Lachlan to stand up and make his way to the bathroom to get dressed. Lachlan laughed on the way. Success!

After Lachlan returned from school he went to the park for a quick turn on the swing. Lachlan has a swing set and a hammock at home but still prefers the ones at the park.

Lachlan ate toast with cheese again tonight which has been one of his goals. How exciting! We left a bowl of strawberries around and hoped Lachlan would eat some, but not today. We will keep on trying. One of these days he will eat them again.

Lachlan fell asleep in less than five minutes this evening, success again!

Wednesday 09/09/15

Lachlan's morning routine went well. When his bus arrived home from school, he looked like he had just woken and seemed tired and hot. He looked unwell around his eyes as they looked heavy. Off we went to see the doctor but when we arrived the doctor's wife told us he had been unwell and was not at work today and she was unsure if he would be back at the surgery the following day.

We decided to call a doctor to the house and Lachlan coped with the examination very well. The doctor examined Lachlan's ears which he did not seem to mind at all. At first he was not keen to have the blood pressure monitor placed on his finger, so the doctor did the rest of the examination first and came back to the blood pressure monitor last and Lachlan was happy with that and accepted the monitor.

The doctor told us Lachlan had croup and gave him a dose of some medication which was put into his juice. Lachlan was not pleased as he could taste the medication in the juice but he reluctantly drank it as knew it was best. In the past Lachlan would not have accepted medication and we have noticed this new positive change within the past year.

Previously he would have run off, or pushed the medication away. When we tried to mix medications with juice Lachlan noticed the colour change of the drink and rejected it. Nowadays Lachlan notices his obviously changed drinks due to supplements but still drinks them.

Thursday 10/09/15

Today Lachlan seemed a little better and he slept well overnight without waking. He played a game in Japanese on the computer and played with Itsal. Around lunchtime Lachlan called me over and pointed out what he had typed into his iPad speaking program. He typed, "I want to go and get a white DVD". I did not know what this meant and I wondered if he meant empty DVD cases, but when I asked him he shook his head.

I asked Lachlan if he was looking for a white DVD from his collection of two hundred or more, but he shook his head and I remembered that he would have known which DVDs in his collection were white because he remembers things like that.

If we were to go shopping for a white DVD, I wanted to make sure it would be available at the first shop we went to as Lachlan was not well enough to walk around between various shops. Being unsure which DVD he wanted I tried to think of a way around this. I found some pictures of various local shopping centres online and he selected one to buy the white DVD from.

When we arrived at the selected shop which had a large range of DVDs, Lachlan went directly to the DVD he wanted and did not look at any others. When he opened the case, the DVD was white.

In the last few weeks Lachlan has started to respond when asked a question by nodding 'yes' and 'no', which is wonderful and very helpful for all of us, especially him. The funny part is he prefers to say no mostly, rather than yes, and I think he is playing it safe. It is fantastic to see him answer questions and make his own choices, (within reason for a nine-year-old).

Susan, a family friend suggested I show Lachlan a YouTube video to explain about medications. I thought this was a good idea and found a cartoon about a little girl who took her medicine and Lachlan laughed as he watched it. He liked to hear the little girl talk from her perspective, as he could relate.

Lachlan had his croup medication mixed in with juice. He understood it was necessary even though he did not really like the taste. At bedtime he fell asleep within a few minutes and so did Itsal.

Lachlan's wetsuit arrived in the mail today which was ordered for his My Choice Matters project, where he will learn to surf in the surf simulator. Lachlan was very interested and excited when he saw it. He will have his first lesson in the coming weeks.

Saturday 12/09/15

Lachlan went to two spring fairs today. The first one was held at the primary school his sister attended when she was younger. Lachlan was reluctant to go inside the gates at first so instead he stood and looked through the fence. When he saw the jumping castle he became eager and wanted to go inside. He had many turns at jumping on the castle and then found dodgem cars and had a ride on those. He also found a DVD which he bought. The second fair had a giant slide which he spent most of his time on and there was also a concert where children danced. He liked their colourful costumes.

Sunday 13/09/15

Lachlan went to a water theme park for the day. When he arrived he pointed out the biggest scariest slide and wanted to go on it. Once he arrived at the top we found he was not tall enough to have a turn on the ride. We did find some other rides for children his age and he was happy with those. On one of the rides he sat on a ring which entered a dark tunnel where water sprayed out and wet him. He loved it.

Monday 14/09/15

Itsal woke me very early as he nudged and licked my arm. When I checked on Lachlan, I noticed his room was very warm but surprisingly Lachlan was still asleep. Itsal wanted to let me know the room had become too warm.

Thursday 17/09/15

Today was a very exciting day as I had some feedback from school who reported that Lachlan had said the words "Boy" and "Hi". At home during the evening I asked Lachlan if he wanted a biscuit and he answered in agreement by nodding. Next I asked him whether he wanted one biscuit or two and he said the word "Two"! There is nothing more exciting around our house than when Lachlan says a word, any word, especially a new one.

Friday 18/09/15

Today was the last day of the school term and Lachlan did not need to wear his school uniform. These days I can explain this to him just by talking about it which has not always been the case. In the past Lachlan became disturbed by the change in routine of wearing different clothes to school as he operated largely on routine. He is much more flexible now.

Lachlan came home with an award from school for cooking, which is something he is not really interested in at home. I guessed he displayed his best behaviour at school, and it was great that he now had this new interest.

Monday 21/09/15

Today Lachlan was very excited after being shown a social story about going to a beach house tomorrow. He helped pack some of his toys and some DVDs which he wanted to take along.

As we packed our belongings Lachlan noticed the large brown freckle near my wrist. The freckle had always been there, but Lachlan may not have noticed it before. He tried to bring my hand to his mouth while he looked for the freckle. For a moment I wondered what he was doing and then I realised he thought my freckle was a chocolate chip. It did look a bit like one and Lachlan loves chocolate chips! When I told him my freckle was not a chocolate chip he laughed a lot.

Lachlan attended a pottery class at a local centre this morning. He really enjoyed being with the other children and making the pottery. He liked handling the clay which was a new experience for him and he followed a series of instructions which were given to him. He was determined to follow all the steps and complete them. He made a duck figurine, and of course Itsal was a big hit with the other children who gave him a lot of attention.

Lachlan was not disturbed at all while he participated in this new activity, in a new place with new people which would not have been possible before Itsal came along. Lachlan has much more confidence in unfamiliar situations now.

After the pottery class we had planned to go to NSW south coast for a short holiday which meant a long period of sitting in the car. It worked out well that Lachlan attended the pottery class first before the long ride. We knew it would be late by the time we arrived at the beach house.

Lachlan was very excited and helped to pack some of his favourite books and DVDs to take to the beach house. Both Lachlan and Itsal were settled in the car during the trip which took five and a half hours. We stopped four times along the way. Long trips were not possible before Itsal came along, but thankfully these days they are. Lachlan was relaxed in the car and even seemed to enjoy the drive.

It was dark when we arrived. The house was elevated with a flight of stairs on the outside which led to the top floor which was the main part of the house. There was a verandah with a dining setting on a deck outside and while I sorted out where the bags were to go, I noticed Lachlan had wandered onto the verandah. Itsal followed Lachlan and also let me know that he had gone outside as he led me by the wrist onto the verandah.

Thursday 24/09/15

Today Lachlan went for a long walk along the boardwalk. He looked at various boats along the way and his steps became faster until he began to run. He ran most of the way until we arrived at a wharf and was really excited when he stood on it and was able to look into the clear water and see oysters and rocks. We found a park along the way and Lachlan had a turn on a spinning wheel ride and a big round swing made of rope. We continued on the boardwalk until we came to a path which led to an inlet.

We walked along the path which had huge rocks on either side of it until we had a clear view of the inlet. The path and rock formation were elevated and Lachlan was able to look down onto the ocean. At times a huge wave would hit the rocks in front of us and spray water over the people who stood there. Lachlan was amused when he got wet and he was in his element as he watched the waves crash onto the rocks.

While we watched the waves we saw a seal swimming in the ocean. Next we saw a dolphin which we pointed out to Lachlan but I was unsure whether he had seen it or not. He seemed to understand it was very special to have seen these animals in the wild.

Friday 25/09/15

Today Lachlan went to visit a gold mining colony. Lachlan liked the gold mine tunnel which he walked up and down several times even though it was dark and cold inside. There was a large water wheel which he stood and watched for some time. The colony had buildings including a chapel, a gaol, a wash house, a post office, a tavern and settler's huts and tents. There was a huge shed full of antique machinery which Lachlan was very interested in. There was also an antique train which he enjoyed looking at.

When we visited the gaol at the gold mining colony I was startled when I saw that it was set up with a mannequin prisoner. The prisoner lay on an antique bed and was clothed in prisoner clothes which were white with black arrows printed on them. He was chained at the ankles. The prisoner's skull was cracked and he had a stern look on his face. As I was the first person in our group to enter the gaol, I wondered whether Lachlan would be scared when he saw the mannequin prisoner, but his reaction to it was quite the opposite.

Lachlan went right over to the prisoner and knocked on his cracked head. Being a little tired he thought he too would have a rest and he laid down with the prisoner in the bed! Lachlan just saw it for what it was, a plastic mannequin laid on a bed, and if you needed to have a rest, well, that was very handy indeed.

This afternoon Lachlan went back to the boardwalk and this time there were two seals on the rocks, and a small dog watched and barked at them. One of the seals looked slightly disturbed and jumped back into the water and swam away. Lachlan was delighted when he saw three beautiful rainbows above the sea and pointed them out to us. He seemed to be enjoying this holiday much more than others he had been on previously.

I remembered a few years ago when we went on holiday and Lachlan did not sleep until 2.00 a.m. as he did not like the unfamiliar bed and surrounds. Even when he finally fell asleep he was in such a light sleep that he woke up several times. He just would not settle and did not seem to enjoy much about that holiday at all.

For the past three nights of this holiday Lachlan had slept peacefully every night without waking, in his own room with Itsal. This evening Lachlan fell asleep in ten minutes.

Sunday 27/09/15

Today we went for a very long walk and followed the beach. On the way back to the beach house we walked across a bridge, a little girl who was also on the bridge told us there was a seal underneath the bridge. We saw it as it turned around and around while it swam. We were very close to it and could see it clearly. Lachlan was excited and we stayed for a long time and watched the seal move around in and out of the water. Lachlan broke off a piece of his bread roll and threw it into the water for the seal.

At bedtime Lachlan seemed a little restless and I fell asleep before he did while I rested in the bed next to his.

Monday 28/09/15

Today we went to the zoo. Once we arrived Lachlan did not want to get out of the car and enter the zoo, as he had something else in mind. We headed back towards the beach house and on the way I asked Lachlan where else he wanted to go. By way of deduction we figured out that he wanted to go to the beach, so we did. Lachlan had a great time as he played in the sand and climbed over the rocks.

In the afternoon we went for a walk in the park and on the way back we stopped on the bridge to look for the seal that we had seen yesterday. The seal was in the exact same place as it was yesterday and Lachlan was very thrilled to see it again. He stood on the bridge for a long time while he looked at the seal from all different angles.

Tonight as usual I laid in the bed next to Lachlan's while he fell asleep. While on holidays Itsal seemed especially protective of Lachlan and wanted to join him on his bed at the same time. At home Itsal usually joins Lachlan on his bed after Lachlan has fallen asleep. This evening Lachlan fell asleep in fifteen minutes.

Tuesday 29/09/15

After a walk on the beach it was time to make the five-hour trip back home. Lachlan was calm and happy on the drive home and Itsal slept at his feet. Lachlan enjoyed looking at the scenery all the way home and did not complain at all. What a huge difference from previous years when the ninety minute drive to his grandma's was more than he could cope with. Having Itsal seems to have made Lachlan much calmer overall. What a wonderful holiday this was with no issues of any kind.

We were amazed that during this holiday Lachlan ate the only type of bread rolls which were available which were totally different to his usual ones. Debbie (speech therapist) has helped Lachlan reach this point as previously he would only eat one type of bread roll, from one bakery. What a long way he has come!

Chapter 10
October 2015

Thursday 01/10/15

Lachlan went to the swim centre today. The centre was quite crowded with children and the noise level made Lachlan slightly disturbed. He held onto my arm for ten minutes which gave him enough time to adjust to the noise level. He was excited when he swam in the wave pool and it did not take long before he led me to the deep end where he could no longer stand and he dodged in and out of the waves.

While swimming today I noticed that Lachlan could quickly exit the pool with ease at all points by pulling himself up onto the sides wherever he wanted to get out. He did this several times while I stayed in the pool and I noticed that he had exited the pool at the exact point which allowed him a view of the surf simulator in action. He was fixated on it for some time and was very excited when I told him that tomorrow it would be his turn to surf on the simulator.

Friday 02/10/15

Lachlan's nanna visited for the day. As soon as she arrived Lachlan gave her a great big bear hug. Occasionally throughout the day Lachlan went over to her and gave her extra hugs. To Lachlan a bear hug is a hug! I worried that Lachlan would squeeze nanna too hard so I reminded him to be gentle. Nanna did not seem to mind and after Lachlan had finished with the hugs he went back to a computer game he had been busy playing and nanna went back to watching the news on television.

This afternoon Lachlan was booked in for his first surfing lesson on the surf simulator. He was very excited after being shown a social story as he knew the lesson would happen today. Leah from the swim centre had phoned to confirm Lachlan's lesson and told us that Jim would be his instructor.

While Lachlan had been waiting for the lesson to start he watched the social story I had made with great delight which showed a video of the surf simulator in action. Lachlan's project will run for six months and was funded by My Choice Matters for people with a disability to achieve some of their goals and dreams. What a fabulous opportunity for Lachlan to achieve his goal of learning to surf by having one on one instruction. Lachlan learns much faster this way.

Lachlan was very excited and he changed into his swimming gear and ran to the door, ready to go. In the car along the way he bounced up and down in the back seat as he was far too excited to sit still. Once we arrived, he raced to the counter and jumped up and down while he waited for the attendant. When Lachlan saw the screen which showed a surfer on the simulator he was even more excited and could hardly wait for his lesson to begin. Leah came to meet us and we walked to the back of the centre where the simulator was situated. When Lachlan met Jim I could tell that he liked him right away.

Lachlan was so excited when water started to gush out of the mesh floor of the simulator and waves formed. He blocked his ears at first as the simulator made a loud noise when it was switched on. After a few seconds Lachlan forgot about the noise when he saw enough water flowing from it to form waves. He jumped up and down with excitement and ran into the waves. He climbed up the mat and slid all the way down the length of it, and for a moment I wondered whether he was slightly hurt as he stopped momentarily and stood still. This happened a few times but Lachlan did not seem concerned at all and kept going back for more.

Lachlan stood on the board briefly in the waves and he seemed to enjoy the harsh sensation of the water pressure on his body and feet even though I had found it slightly uncomfortable. Towards the end of the lesson Jim re-entered the simulator and Lachlan watched him intently as he surfed. Jim made it look easy!

Next Lachlan had a swim in one of the warm indoor pools to warm himself up as he was a little cold. Next lesson we may take Lachlan's wetsuit which was bought for this project by My Choice Matters.

Back at home Lachlan watched each one of the videos I had taken of him as he surfed. He jumped up and down excitedly and seemed proud of himself as he pointed out his favourite parts of the videos. He was in an extremely happy mood for the rest of the evening.

Sunday 04/10/15

After he played with Itsal most of the morning, Lachlan and I headed out shopping. Lachlan looked at DVDs, toys, books and surfboards. He insisted that I buy three bottles of water, all the same brand with different coloured lids. I had no idea why. After we bought the water bottles Lachlan led me to the food court where we sat. Lachlan was not interested in eating any food there certainly not unusual take away food and not even his own favourite bread rolls which we had taken along. This was all very unusual as Lachlan tends not to be interested in sitting in the food court usually. Next Lachlan took the three water bottles from the bag and placed them on the table side by side and insisted I open them all and try them.

The food court was filled with people and some watched Lachlan as he tried the flavoured waters. He seemed surprised about the different tastes of each, but seemed to like them. We stayed for fifteen minutes while Lachlan pointed at the bottles and although he expected a response from me, I was unsure of exactly what he had tried to communicate. Lachlan was very pleased when I also tried the different flavours and some onlookers who had been eating lunch were very amused. The things we do as parents!

Next we went to an electronic shop to buy a computer cord. Lachlan looked at the computers and I think he remembered there had been some talk of him getting a new computer in the near future. He pointed to a brand name on one of the computers which let me know the preferred brand of his next computer. I did not know why he selected that particular brand as it was different to the one he used at home. I told him that we were not buying the computer today and then he looked at digital frames and I told him we were not buying those either, just the cord on this trip. Lachlan looked around the shop a little more before we left to go home.

Monday 05/10/15

Today we visited some relatives. Lachlan was interested in having a swim but was reluctant as there were more people than usual in the pool area and surrounds. This naturally meant there was more noise than at other times in the past when he had been swimming in the same pool.

Lachlan played at the edge of the pool and various people (including myself) tried to encourage him to enter the pool. People who did not know him asked whether he was able to swim and some assumed that he could not which was the reason for his reluctance. People who were familiar with Lachlan knew there must have been another reason for his reluctance.

Dad often swims with Lachlan, but as he was not there today I went into the pool thinking this might encourage Lachlan to join me. He seemed slightly pleased that I had got into the pool and handed me a surfboard, although he was not convinced he should do the same.

Throughout the day Lachlan played at the edge of the pool and tested the water with his feet every now and then. He threw his drink bottle into the pool several times and his good-natured cousin Jai, retrieved it several times for him. Lachlan seemed to enjoy that game which was his way of playing with his third cousin whom he had met for the first time today.

Lachlan is very fond of his cousin Dan's friend whose name is also Dan. Every time Lachlan saw him he wanted to play rough with him. Lachlan grabbed his hair a few times and gestured to be picked up and pointed to the pool. Dan carried Lachlan (which was not easy to do) to the pool area as he requested but Lachlan was not yet ready go into the water.

After most of the visitors had left at the end of the day and the pool was empty, Lachlan decided to have a swim as I think he had found the noise level too high earlier in the day.

Tuesday 06/10/15

When we arrived at the shops today Lachlan clearly said the word "Wire" for the first time. As I wondered why, Lachlan walked over to a wire fence at the rear of the car park and looked into a storm water drain behind the wire fence. There was a small stream of dirty water with some rubbish around it but to Lachlan it might have been a potential swimming or surfing site. The colour of the water and the rubbish were not a problem to him!

Once inside the shopping centre Lachlan saw a children's ride. A little boy sat on the ride as it turned around and he began talking to Lachlan. The boy did not seem to mind that he received no obvious answer back from Lachlan immediately. Lachlan communicated in his own way with the boy as he chased him around on the ride while the little boy laughed loudly and continued to talk to Lachlan.

The boy's parents who had been watching, suggested that Lachlan join their son on the ride, so Lachlan jumped on. Both boys laughed as the little boy started to sing a song which Lachlan thought was hilarious.

We have found that most children do not seem to mind that Lachlan does not talk to them, although many children ignore him. Occasionally he comes across a child who shows a particular interest in him and will go out of their way to include him.

During Lachlan's evening routine he has been brushing his teeth for part of the count down from one hundred to one. This time he had continued for the whole of the countdown which made it the first time Lachlan brushed his teeth independently. Persevering had paid off. Great work Lachlan!

Wednesday 07/10/15

Today was the first day back at school. Lachlan seemed happy to be going back school and I think he was looking forward to seeing his friends. There was a new assistant in the school bus, which would have disturbed him once, but today Lachlan was unconcerned about the change. These changes have probably helped Lachlan learn to become more flexible.

Thursday 08/10/15

At the dentist today I picked up some toothpaste which was recommended for Lachlan as it contains calcium which Lachlan lacks as he does not drink milk. Lachlan has a calcium supplement added to his dinner instead, but when he does not eat all of his dinner he misses out on calcium so the toothpaste should be very helpful for him if he accepts it.

The toothpaste had a hot minty taste. I blended it with his usual toothpaste to minimise the hot minty taste and Lachlan did not notice the difference or if he did, he did not mind. Fantastic that he accepted it so easily!

We tried to offer Lachlan cheese slices and sticks but since being sick a few weeks ago, he was now reluctant to even touch them. He had gradually increased the amount of dinner he ate since he was sick and now was almost back to eating his usual amount. Lately he has been interested in eating chocolate koalas and has requested them for the last two nights. He allowed them to melt in his hands while he ate them (messy!), but we were very pleased that he had tried and enjoyed a new food even if it was chocolate.

Friday 09/10/15

After a happy and successful day at school we head off for a surfing lesson (Lachlan's My Choice Matters project). Lachlan was very happy when he arrived and saw Jim surfing in the big waves.

Lachlan walked around the sides and above the simulator as he warmed himself to the idea of the waves. I felt slightly anxious as I watched him climb up the walls like a superhero, as I knew they were very slippery. Lachlan climbed to the top several times and slipped and slid down the entire length of the simulator without any reluctance at all. He was having the time of his life and kept going back for more. Most of the lesson was spent sliding up and down the wall and in and out of the water and Lachlan seemed to delight in the sensation it gave him.

This evening Lachlan handed me a wrapper from a chocolate he had previously eaten and enjoyed. He had kept the wrapper somewhere and now had bought it to me as a way to request the same chocolate again. Amazing that he always finds ways to communicate his wants.

Saturday 10/10/15

Lachlan clearly indicted he wanted to visit the fish markets. While in the car he pointed in the direction he wanted us to follow and the final destination was the fish markets. He had never visited the fish markets before so we were not sure what he had expected to see there. It was very noisy and crowded inside but Lachlan was excited and quickly darted in and out of the shops as he briefly inspected them. He enjoyed seeing different shops with various types of fish and seafood and he especially liked seeing one of the workers in a shop grilling oysters with a hand torch.

Lachlan was not interested in eating any of food from the fish market himself, although he seemed mildly interested that other people were. I wondered what he would think if he knew that sometimes he did eat pureed fish in his dinner but could not taste it.

Sunday 11/10/15

Today was Lachlan's soccer presentation. We arrived just in time as the presentation was about to start. Lachlan was excited when he saw the table with all the trophies on it as he knew he would receive one. All the children in the team sat on a bench and each waited for their turn to receive their trophies. Lachlan was too excited to sit still and wait on the bench, so he stood with me. The crowd of people, noise and the excitement made him want to run off, more with his own excitement than with fear. Lachlan waited to the side of the main crowd until his name was called and when he was presented with his trophy (now his third) he held onto it and jumped around with excitement. I offered to hold it for him while he played but he wanted to hold it himself as he was so proud of it.

Tuesday 13/10/15

This morning there was a consultation with Debbie (Speech therapist) regarding Lachlan's food issues. Some of the goals for the month were to try garlic bread, bacon, sausages and continue toast with cheese.

Wednesday 14/10/15

This evening I made toast with cheese as part of Lachlan's food plan and left it on a plate near Lachlan hoping he would be interested. I offered it to him twice and he placed it back onto the plate and left it. About half an hour later I watched as he held the toast and brushed it on his cheek. Then he looked at the cheese, touched it and turned the toast over to the opposite side where there was no cheese and picked off some toast from there and ate it. Then he picked off some cheese but placed it on the floor.

Next I noticed that while he ate the next pieces of toast he placed less of the cheese on the floor, and when he ate the next piece of toast he ate most of the cheese. Fantastic!

Lately we have noticed that Lachlan now eats and drinks together when he had not done this previously. In the past Lachlan would only either eat or drink, one at a time. It is fantastic to see these changes!

Thursday 15/10/15

Lachlan was thrilled once again when he arrived for his lesson and saw Jim surfing in the big waves making it look like anyone could have easily done the same. Lachlan followed the waves with his hands, pointing at them and moving them up and down with the rhythm of the waves which indicated his interest and focus. This is one of the ways Lachlan communicates that he approves or likes an activity. During this lesson Lachlan held onto the surfboard more than he did at his previous lesson and seemed to be getting used to the idea that the board should stay with him while he slid down the slippery blue mat. He stayed and played in the water most of the lesson and slid up and down the mat which Jim told us people often learned last rather than at the start of lessons.

This evening after the surfing lesson Lachlan seemed quite tired.

As part of his food plan I placed a hot dog on a plate in Lachlan's view and left it to see if Lachlan would show an interest as he had been mildly interested in them in the past. I could not believe that after he looked at it a few times he touched the sausage which had tomato sauce on it. Next he picked off a piece of the bread and gave it to me to eat. After I ate it he went back and picked off another piece of the bread from the hotdog and this time ate it himself. He continued to eat the bread and then picked up the sausage, touched it to his cheek and smelt it. Next he put it back on the plate and did not eat it.

He did eat most of the hot dog roll however, and then asked for another one. It was unbelievable to us that he tried it the first time he had seen it at home. I wondered if he had noticed children enjoying them at parties or at school which had made him interested in them.

Friday 16/10/15

Today we had a very successful day, food wise. At dinner time I left two cheese rolls which I had bought from a local bakery on a plate near Lachlan. Lachlan did not want to eat his usual pureed food and chose the cheese rolls instead! Marvellous!

These cheese rolls were different to others Lachlan had seen at home so we did not expect he would eat them. We would have been happy for him to have tolerated the cheese rolls on a plate in the same room as him, so we were excited when we saw him pick one up and eat the cheese from the top of it! I could hardly believe it when Lachlan ate the second cheese roll. We wondered if he would want more than two so we went to buy more of them. The ones we had bought earlier had run out so we bought some similar ones but Lachlan did not want to eat them as they were a lighter colour and slightly different shape. To him they were very different!

Lachlan was still hungry so he ate more toast with cheese and at times picked off some of the cheese and gave it to me or put it onto his plate. Persevering has paid off.

Sunday 18/10/15

Lachlan used his iPad to request a trip to the shopping centre as he wanted to look at children's rides. Once we were there I remembered that Lachlan needed some new shoes and thought it was a good opportunity to buy some, but I knew Lachlan probably would not feel the same way. I explained to him that we needed to buy shoes and we headed in in the direction of the shoe shop. Instead of going the way I asked, he led me inside a major department store. He seemed to know where he was leading me and we went up the escalator, up and down isles, in and out and up and down, so much so that I wondered where we would end up. We came to the store exit which was now on another level to the one we entered the store on. However, it was a bit closer to the shoe shop so that worked out well.

Next Lachlan walked past another large department store before he stopped and led me inside that store. I told him that we needed to go to the shoe shop and promised him we would look at things he was interested in afterwards. He still insisted that I follow him into the department store. He did the same thing again, led me up, down and around the store. I asked him if he wanted to look at toys and he shook his head and kept walking. I had no idea what he was looking for in the store and I wondered whether he was confused. He still insisted I follow him around the store which I did until eventually we came to the store exit, which was very close to the shoe store! I had no idea how he knew where all the twists and turns would lead us as I had never taken him that way before.

When we arrived at the shoe store loud music played inside and Lachlan blocked his ears. The sales assistant noticed Lachlan was slightly distressed and turned the music down. She showed us the children's shoes and I asked Lachlan to choose from the selection.

At that point I remembered my handbag contained a drawing which was an outline of Lachlan's feet in order to buy the correct size shoes (should I have come across them when Lachlan was not with me), so I gave this to the sales assistant for sizing.

Lachlan pointed to a plain black pair of shoes and the sales assistant went to find the right size for him. At this point it was clear that Lachlan wanted to buy the shoes and leave as he was still uncomfortable about the loud music. We quickly paid for the shoes and left the store.

We went to look at DVDs in Lachlan's favourite shop. He looked at DVDs for quite a long time and knew exactly where all his favourite brands were positioned. He chose some DVDs from different shelves and sections and walked around with them while he looked at others. When I asked him to return them to the shelves he remembered the exact position of each one.

Saturday 24/10/15

While Lachlan ate his breakfast, he watched some French and Spanish YouTube videos. I noticed they were of DVDs which he had English versions of in his own collection. He always remembers the path to locate videos which interest him, so only needs to search once.

On his way out the door this morning Lachlan grabbed the apple that I had left on a plate for him yesterday, and took it with him. He had never done this before so I thought he may eat the apple. He held onto it for quite some time in the car and when the car door opened, he dropped it and it bruised. Lachlan noticed that the apple now felt different and no longer wanted to hold it.

We went to an Indian culture festival. When Lachlan arrived he marched around as though he was looking for something. One of the stallholders noticed him and thought he looked like he was on a mission as he marched around looking at the various stalls and games.

There were many food and games stalls. One of the games stalls had an interactive screen and Lachlan knew how it worked as soon as he saw it. He jumped on a castle and a group of eight boys who knew each other and were slightly older than Lachlan, began to talk to him. We watched carefully to make sure no bullying occurred, but these children were very friendly and kind to Lachlan. They asked him questions such as what his name was, how old he was and which school he attended. We often respond on Lachlan's behalf by telling children that Lachlan does not talk very much, but this time we were a little too far away so we watched and listened instead.

We noticed that when Lachlan did not respond verbally to the boys they just said, "OK then, let's jump," and Lachlan and the boys forgot about talking and jumped and played together. Lachlan was happy!

Sunday 25/10/15

This morning Lachlan played on the computer and when I entered the room he said, "Hey mum," and pulled me towards the computer to show me a YouTube video of a steam train he had found. I was so excited to hear him call out to me for the first time that I became stunned and statue like as I tried to pretend I was not surprised that he had spoken. I followed my gut feeling and made no noticeable reaction as I did not want to alarm him. Most times I respond by telling him that I like his talking.

Samantha came to visit and watched Lachlan as he amused himself in the spa. He played with a bucket which was not a toy but a full-size bucket which he would fill, lift up and tip back into the spa. Samantha noticed how strong he was as he lifted the full bucket so easily.

Samantha kindly took Itsal to the vet for his yearly vaccination and check-up. The vet told her Itsal was in perfect shape and that he had lost just a small amount of weight since he was last seen, one year ago.

This afternoon Lachlan played outside with Itsal. He chased Itsal who had a stick in his mouth. It was impossible to catch Itsal as we chased him with the stick. He raced around in circles very fast and I have not found a person able to catch him yet!

Wednesday 28/10/15

This evening we heard and saw some fireworks in the sky which were nearby and most likely part of an event at the local school. Lachlan watched them from the verandah and stood on a chair to have a better view. He jumped up and down as he was excited when he saw the different colours and patterns which appeared in the sky. At times he traced an outline of the shape the fireworks made in the sky with his finger.

When the display finished he waited for a few moments and hoped they would restart but understood when they didn't, even though he would have loved to have seen more. Itsal did not seem frightened by the fireworks, unlike other dogs I had seen. After the firework display Itsal led me by my wrist to his food bowl and reminded me that his dinner was late.

Friday 30/10/15

Lachlan finds anything to do with Halloween funny. I showed him a gingerbread cookie which I had bought which had a face with fangs on it, and he was quite interested in it. He unwrapped it and scratched it with his nails several times to check the hardness of it. We were pleased he showed interest in the cookie and hoped he would also be interested in other foods. He held onto the cookie for some time and took it into his room when it was time for his bedtime routine. As I told him a story I had made up about Halloween, he broke the little white fangs off the cookie and placed them in my mouth. Then he said "treat" for the first time.

Next he broke off four little pink buttons from the cookie, and I ate those as well. Next an arm and then another arm and Lachlan became a little upset because I could not eat them as fast as he would have liked. The legs followed, then the body which he wanted me to eat. He tested the cookie out on me first but he did not eat any of it. Well, maybe next time.

Saturday 31/10/15

Lachlan slept in and woke when he was ready which was ninety minutes later than he woke on school days. He knew when he woke up without Itsal's help that it was not a school day, if he didn't know already.

Lachlan played on the computer while he ate his breakfast and when I noticed crumbs on the carpet I bought out the vacuum cleaner to clean them. When Lachlan was a toddler he needed to be outside the house before vacuuming could be done as he was so sensitive to the noise, it was unbearable for him. He slowly became used to the sound over the years which started by using the vacuum in another room for short periods of time and building it up from there.

It helped when Lachlan had some control over when the vacuum cleaner started. I showed him the vacuum cleaner and asked him to say "Go" when I started it, which gave him some control over it. I showed him how to turn the vacuum on and off so that when the noise became unbearable he could turn it off if he needed to. It is lucky that Lachlan does not like mess in his room or anywhere else in the house and whenever I ask him if he thinks we should use the vacuum cleaner, he always agrees.

This afternoon, Lachlan dressed up in a zombie outfit to go out to a Halloween party with his sister Samantha which was to be held at a local school. Samantha told me that when they arrived at the party, Lachlan had changed his mind and decided to sit in the car instead. Samantha then asked him if he wanted to go visit his favourite shops as an alternative and he nodded, so off they went.

As Samantha and Lachlan walked into the shopping centre they passed by a large garbage bin and heard something rustling around inside it. They looked inside the bin and found two tiny black and white kittens. The kittens looked healthy and had been playing inside the bin. Samantha picked the kittens up and took them back to her car where they sat with Lachlan on the back seat during the ride home. Samantha told me that Lachlan seemed to like them and thankfully they were not frightened of him either.

Samantha has always been interested in animals and occasionally takes care of stray or abandoned animals needing help (through a rescue service), so she took the kittens' home and was to have them checked by the vet and find for suitable homes for them.

Chapter 11
November 2015

Sunday 01/11/15

This morning I woke at 4.30 a.m. as I heard Lachlan had woken in his room. Itsal was sitting next to my bed and licked my hand to make sure I was awake and knew Lachlan was up and about. A few minutes later Lachlan came in and turned on my bedroom light and then ran off back to his own room. Lachlan went and got his DVD player and watched a DVD in his room and did not go back to sleep.

Later on in the morning we went to the newsagent and enquired about a DVD which we had ordered. The shop assistant gave Lachlan the DVD but Lachlan was unhappy as it was somehow different to what he expected, even though it was the one we had ordered. Lachlan stomped his foot down hard on the ground in protest but reluctantly signed "Thank you" to the shop assistant when asked.

Kitten update; Samantha took the kittens to see the vet who told her one of the kittens had a heart murmur but seemed to be in good health and would need to be checked again in a few weeks. The kittens were also covered in fleas and their skin was in poor condition so they received some treatment and Samantha planned to keep them for a few weeks and find a suitable home for them when they were ready.

This evening Lachlan brushed his teeth independently while I counted to one hundred. I reminded him to brush each section and in the last ten seconds of the countdown I took over to make sure the teeth at the front had been brushed properly. Fantastic!

Monday 02/11/15

This evening I placed some strawberries on a plate near Lachlan (and hoped that he would start eating them again). He looked at them a few times but did not seem interested in trying them. I placed a strawberry on his computer table as I knew it would be in his way and he would need to move it in order to use the computer. There had been times in the past when his interest had been sparked after he had touched foods, but this time he just put the strawberry back onto the plate with the others.

This is the opposite of when he was a toddler and had been obsessed with strawberries. We would go to shops all over looking for them as we needed to have them available at home at all times in case Lachlan wanted them.

Lachlan has only ever eaten a very small selection of foods so we made sure we always had strawberries available. We never really know which food is going to be the next big thing of interest to him. Debbie told us that Lachlan would most likely go back to eating things he had eaten previously. We have seen this also, so will keep trying with the strawberries.

Tuesday 03/11/15

Lachlan arrived as usual in the school bus this afternoon. I opened the side door and Lachlan stepped out of the bus. While we waited for the driver to get Lachlan's school bag from the back of the bus all of a sudden Lachlan touched the inside of one of the wheels on the bus. I told him to stop but it was too late as he had already touched it. At first I thought he may have burned his finger but he did not seem hurt, just a little upset as I had raised my voice when I told him not to touch the wheel. His finger seemed fine and I was glad he had not been injured!

I remembered once a few years back when Lachlan and I had been grocery shopping. When we arrived home I carried several shopping bags and went to walk up the steps into the front door. I asked Lachlan a few times to come inside with me but he wanted to stay with the car. The bags were heavy so I walked towards the steps which led onto the front verandah and hoped Lachlan would follow me- but he didn't, he just stayed near the car. I did not want to go inside and lose sight of Lachlan, so I called him again from the verandah. He looked up at me and then bent down and touched the exhaust pipe on the car. I thought he would have been injured as I assumed it was hot, but I was amazed that he was not hurt at all. Lucky!

This evening while Lachlan played in his room with Itsal he said the word "Tail" for the first time! We often tell Lachlan not to touch Itsal's tail so maybe this was the reason.

Thursday 05/11/15

Itsal woke me just before it was time for my wake-up alarm to sound. He led me by the hand to Lachlan's room and I noticed Lachlan had kicked his blankets off and may have been cold. Itsal also wanted to go outside to the toilet but usually waits until someone opens the back door for some reason and then takes the opportunity to go outside. Rarely, he has led me by the hand to the back door when he needed to go outside immediately and strangely enough he has never asked anybody else.

Itsal will also lead me by the hand, away from the door and any danger, if he hears or senses something or someone outside which is of concern to him. When Lachlan and Itsal are alone in a room, Itsal is aware that he is the only one protecting Lachlan and his reaction to a person or potential threat outside is much stronger. He will bark loudly to warn them off and also to alert me and he will sit in front of Lachlan to prevent him moving. He will not allow anyone to come close to Lachlan and is able to read each situation and change his reaction to suit.

I remembered once when the school bus arrived early and the assistant had come up to the front door while I was busy in another room. I had never seen Itsal make such a strong reaction. He barked furiously at the assistant who came up to the door and called out to Lachlan. Itsal had reacted this way as he knew I did not see the person at the door and therefore he was the only one responsible for protecting Lachlan.

Friday 06/11/15

Lachlan likes Fridays as it is swimming day at school and he also has a surfing lesson after school. Lachlan missed the last two weeks of surfing lessons as he had been a bit unwell with a persistent cough. When he arrived for the lesson he was so happy which he indicated by jumping up and down with excitement. Lachlan warmed up to the lesson and he walked around the outside of the surf simulator. Once he warmed up he sat on the board and enjoyed the strong water pressure as it increased. I wondered how Lachlan was able to stay on the surfboard as I was amazed that the pressure of the water did not pull him off the board. He just sat there and seemed to enjoy the strong sensation of it. When the water pressure became extremely high it made much more noise and Lachlan blocked his ears with his fingers, still managing to stay in the waves somehow. He had a fantastic time and did extremely well.

Saturday 07/11/15

Today is Lachlan's nanna's 80th birthday party. Nanna came to our house in the morning and Lachlan was very pleased to see her as usual. I am sure Lachlan remembers the bond they shared before dementia took over. Every now and then Lachlan gave nanna a bear hug and was reminded to "be gentle". Nanna did not seem to mind the bear hugs and I think she was glad Lachlan wanted to interact with her. We all travelled to the party location and when we arrived Lachlan headed to the cabinet where the DVDs were kept to check out the collection there. Afterwards he swam in the pool with his cousin Steven where they stayed until it was time to sing 'Happy Birthday'. The party entertainers Ross and Stephanie sang the birthday song as Lachlan watched. We noticed he had also watched Ross and Stephanie's performance from the pool. Lachlan likes guitars and he watched Ross intently as he played.

One of Lachlan's older cousins, Nathan, travelled from Queensland where he had been working, to attend the party. Lachlan has not seen him for many months and acknowledged him by approaching him and bumping his head slightly against Nathan's in a playful manner. Lachlan did not interact with other people at the party as he preferred to swim in the pool with his cousin, Steven.

Lachlan did not eat cake or any party food. He preferred the bread rolls bought from home, the same as usual.

Monday 09/11/15

This evening while Lachlan laid on his bed during his wind down routine he signed "More" and gestured by touching my fingers. He held my hand and tried to separate my thumb and finger and signed "More" again. As I tried to figure out what he was asking he grabbed my hand, separated my fingers once more and put my hand on his leg. He signed "More" again and now I knew what he wanted! He wanted me to massage his legs. Perhaps he had growing pains. After I massaged his legs he became very relaxed and slept well overnight.

Wednesday 11/11/15

As a usual part of the morning routine Itsal and I woke Lachlan by switching on his DVD player. Itsal jumped on and off the bed and found some gaps in Lachlan's clothes where he nudged and licked him a few times. I reminded Lachlan of the day of the week and told him that it was a good day so that he would expect the same, but he likes Fridays best.

Itsal and I tried a few times to raise Lachlan from his bed and I told him again it was Wednesday, a school day, and he responded by placing his head underneath the pillow. Itsal had another idea and picked up Lachlan's homework sheet and jumped onto the bed with it in his mouth and gave it to Lachlan. This was Itsal's way of getting his message across to Lachlan that it was a school day!

After I moved the DVD player out of Lachlan's room and changed the DVD Lachlan decided he would get out of bed and change it to one he preferred. Lachlan will often get out of bed it he hears the DVD change.

Lachlan seemed aware that the school bus was running slightly late and he wanted to go and wait outside for it to arrive. There were some workers landscaping the newly built house next door and Lachlan ran over to see what they were doing. He liked seeing them paint and busily work on the new house. Lachlan was happy when the bus arrived a few minutes later.

Thursday 12/11/15

Lachlan woke around 4.00 a.m. and a short while after he started to play with Itsal in his bedroom. I heard him laughing and having a great old time. One hour later he settled down and went back to sleep. He did not seem to mind being woken by Itsal when it was time for school even though he must have been very tired.

This evening Lachlan agreed to hold a cheese stick. Half an hour later he was still holding it and I saw him rolling it up and down his cheek. This was exactly what we had hoped as it was getting closer to his mouth.

Lachlan was tired this evening from waking during the early hours and did not want to play in his room as usual. He went straight into bed and placed his head underneath the pillow which meant he wanted to go to sleep and fifteen minutes later he fell asleep.

Friday 13/11/15

Lachlan went for his surfing lesson this afternoon. There had been a storm and we were unsure whether or not the lesson would have to be postponed, but luckily there had not been too much lightening, so the surf simulator could still be operated.

It was still raining a little and it was slightly colder than usual in the surf simulator, but this did not stop Lachlan from having fun. He ran around the edge of the simulator before he slid down part the mat which was outside the water several times. Next he moved into the water section and slid down the length of the mat. He sat on the surfboard while Jim turned up the water pressure and Lachlan became more and more excited as the wave size and pressure increased. This evening there were a few spectators from around the swim centre who watched Lachlan.

After the surfing lesson we went for a swim in the pools at the swim centre. At first Lachlan went into the toddler pool to warm himself up. He was very pleased when he noticed a little girl doing exactly the same thing as him right next to him, which was lying on her back in a floating position. The girl started copying all of Lachlan's movements and they both started laughing. These days Lachlan enjoys playing with other children which is a change from when he was much younger when I often wondered whether he would ever engage with other children. It is wonderful to see that now he does.

After we had been in the deep pool for a while Lachlan noticed that I had been following him but not really swimming myself. Lachlan signed the "More" sign and for a moment I wondered what he wanted more of. At first I thought that he was asking for more time in the pool. Then Lachlan moved my arms to and fro, twice, which indicated that he wanted me to swim. He noticed I was not having enough fun!

Saturday 14/11/15

Today I made a gingerbread house and gingerbread man for Lachlan. He held onto the gingerbread man for a long time and I knew that meant he would be likely to eat it. After about two hours I noticed the gingerbread man's legs were missing and I assumed he had eaten them. It seems the time for him to get used to new foods is becoming shorter!

When Lachlan had a bath this evening Itsal became concerned which had not happened before. For some reason Itsal was concerned about Lachlan being by himself in the bathroom this evening, so I encouraged him to go and sit with Lachlan while he took his bath.

Sunday 15/11/15

Lachlan and I started a pillow fight which Lachlan loved. He laughed a lot and requested "More" several times before Itsal came into the room. When Itsal saw the pillow fight, he grabbed onto my wrist with his mouth and tried to lead me away from Lachlan. It seemed he did not like the idea of the pillow fight. However, Lachlan signed "More" and we started the pillow fight again.

While the pillow fight continued, Itsal waited for the first opportunity to seize my wrist and this time led me out of the room and away from Lachlan. Now I was sure he did not like the pillow fight. Lachlan continued to roll around and play on the bed. He laid on the edge of the bed and hung over the side a little which Itsal noticed even before I had a chance to do anything. Itsal nudged Lachlan a few times which forced him to move back fully onto the bed.

After a quiet day at home we went to visit Samantha for a birthday celebration in the afternoon and both Lachlan and Itsal were very pleased to see her. We noticed the two little black and white kittens had grown, and one of them remembered Lachlan and approached him. The kittens were not frightened of Itsal at all and one of them approached him as he lay down in the position where he was asked to stay. Itsal looked slightly wary of the kitten, but he did not move or make any response to it.

While dinner was being prepared Lachlan covered his ears to block out the loud noise from the food blender. As he was unable to block it out completely and was still disturbed by it, I suggested he play outside for a while until the blender stopped. I knew that Lachlan would not eat the delicious dinner which was being prepared; chicken with coconut strawberry sauce and rice, so I had bought along his usual bread and cheese.

Lachlan would not eat the bread and cheese, maybe because it was given to him at a different location or perhaps because he was too excited. Later in the evening he decided to eat a bread roll.

Monday 16/11/15

This afternoon after school we went to one of the local parks. Lachlan spent a long time on the swing and signed "More" as to be wanted to be pushed as high as possible. It is surprising just how high he is able to go without holding on to the swing, not falling off. Lachlan laughed loudly as he watched two children who played with the water bubbler after their parents had called them away.

Lachlan played on the large castle in the rope tunnel and did not mind that I asked him to wait while a much younger boy went first. While Lachlan sat in the rope tunnel and waited while a little girl around four years of age sat closely behind him. The girl spoke to Lachlan and although I could not understand her words, Lachlan and the girl worked it out between themselves and the two of them laughed as they moved along the tunnel together.

In between turns on the swing Lachlan laid on the ground, probably because the rubber flooring under the swings was warm from the sun and he enjoyed the feeling of the wind on his face.

Tuesday 17/11/15

This morning Itsal and I started the morning routine of waking Lachlan. I placed the DVD player in his room and a few minutes later Itsal jumped onto Lachlan's bed and nudged him on his arm twice. Next he nudged Lachlan's feet. Lachlan shuffled around and hid underneath his pillow and after that Itsal did something I had not seen before. He picked up Lachlan's blanket with his mouth and tried to uncover Lachlan so that he would get out of bed!

I have the task of feeding Itsal in the mornings and it is Lachlan's job to feed him in the evenings. This morning when I fed him he sat and stared at me. I did not know why he was hesitant to eat his food, so I encouraged him to eat it but again he just sat and stared at me. Next Itsal drew my attention to his empty feeding cup- as he stared at it, and I realised what he had noticed.

I had not placed Itsal's feeding cup back in the usual spot on the table like Lachlan always does as I had placed it on a kitchen stool instead. Once I moved the feeding cup back to the usual place, Itsal ate his food. Itsal and Lachlan both like things done the same way each time.

Friday 18/11/15

Lachlan was very excited about the school excursion today to a neighbouring school for a Gala Day. The highlight for Lachlan was a helicopter which landed in front of children and they got the opportunity to go inside it. Lachlan also liked seeing Santa. I was unsure whether Lachlan thought he was too old for Santa. Apparently not, he still liked him.

This afternoon Lachlan went to his surfing lesson at the surf simulator. It was an extremely hot afternoon at forty-two degrees Celsius. When we arrived at the swim centre the car park was full as it was such a hot day, so we parked in a nearby street. We walked to the swim centre as fast as we could to avoid the staying in the hot weather.

Lachlan waited for the lesson to start and once it did neither Lachlan or Itsal seemed bothered by the hot weather. Lachlan was ready to go into the waves and went straight in without any hesitation. He slid up and down on the mat in the waves and ran through the water. He sat on the board in the waves and when Jim turned up the water pressure to high, Lachlan left the waves temporarily due to the noise rather than the water. When he re-entered the water he was in his element, his favourite thing, and he was maybe the happiest he could be.

Saturday 21/11/15

Lachlan went surfing at the beach today. The beach was perfect for him as it had small even waves. He sat on his surf board steadily and stayed on it in the waves. He had the time of his life and after about ninety minutes we thought it best to leave as it had become cold and Lachlan did not have his wetsuit with him.

Next we visited nanna Betty where Lachlan did his routine as usual and looked through nanna's DVD collection until he found some he wanted to watch. He interacted with nanna every now and then over lunch.

Sunday 22/11/15

Itsal woke me at 5.00 a.m. by nudging my arm several times. When I woke I heard Lachlan playing in his room. He was happy enough as he played by himself and did not go back to sleep.

Later on that morning we went shopping and Lachlan picked out some blue Christmas bauble decorations for our Christmas tree. Lachlan was very excited as he decorated it when he saw and remembered decorations he had made from previous years.

Monday 23/11/15

When I woke Lachlan, I noticed a Daddy Long-Legs spider above his head, on the bed head. After I pointed the spider out to Lachlan, I asked him to get out of bed and move away from it. Instead, Lachlan moved his hand toward the spider and when I told him not to touch it, he seemed upset. He is not frightened of spiders or bugs, quite the opposite; he always wants to pick them up.

At news time at school Lachlan used his iPad and told everyone about how he had decorated the Christmas tree and I was glad he chose that topic instead of talking about the spider. Wonderful that he is able to share his news through his iPad each week. He often shares surfing news and photos so perhaps it was good he shared something different as some of the other children may not be as interested in surfing as him.

Tuesday 24/11/15

This evening while Lachlan listened to music in his room he pointed to the place on his bed where Itsal usually slept. I knew that this meant he wanted Itsal who was somewhere else in the house, so I asked Lachlan to go and find him. Using no words, I wondered how Lachlan would be able to instruct Itsal to follow him, but they both returned together walking side by side. Somehow the two of them are able to communicate their needs to each other. I was unsure if Lachlan was able to command Itsal or whether Itsal knew instinctively what Lachlan wanted.

Friday 27/11/15

Today at the surfing lesson Lachlan walked and ran around the outside of the surf simulator as he warmed himself to the idea of entering the water. He preferred to get wet bit by bit rather than all at once. The water was slightly heated in the simulator but felt cold at times due to the weather outside. Jim turned up the wave pressure in the simulator and Lachlan became captivated by the waves and entered the water. There was no stopping him and eventually Jim turned the simulator up to full throttle. Lachlan seemed to enjoy the wave pressure and ran in and out of the waves continuously. At times Lachlan sat down to absorb the full impact of the waves on his body. For Lachlan, this was happiness!

Saturday 28/11/15

We are always looking for ways to incorporate other activities into Lachlan's outings in order to help him understand the need to share his time and consider other people's needs. Today's outing involved going to a new shopping centre and for Chris and Lachlan to meet up with Chris' best friend Ross whom they had not seen for some time. It would be a test to see if such outings would work in the future. The plan was to allow Lachlan to look around all the shops and rides as usual and then have some sit down time at lunch time and chat to Ross. Lachlan was very accommodating and this worked well for everyone. You could say it was a win-win-win situation. Lachlan went on some rides and looked in the shop and he listened to Ross when he tried to engage with him.

Lachlan seemed to enjoy sitting and chatting at lunchtime. When Ross left he shook hands with Chris and Lachlan decided that it was appropriate to join in so placed his hand on theirs. Ross and Chris were very pleased at his willingness to be involved. Lachlan continued to look around the shops until he saw the ramp which led to the car park and then decided to head in that direction as he signed "Finished".

Next Lachlan was given the option of going either to the airport to look at airplanes, or the park to play. He chose the airport and when they arrived he and his Dad parked near the runway to get a really close look at the planes. Lachlan was overjoyed when the first big jet took off a few hundred meters away.

Lachlan pointed at it the plane as it rose higher and followed it with his finger until it was a faint blur in the sky. Another plane departed and others landed. Lachlan explored the area nearby and looked for more wonders. He looked closely at some parked planes and asked Dad to take him to them and when he found out he could go no closer he decided it was time to go.

Sunday 29/11/15

Lachlan joined a junior surfing group today. It was an early start but Lachlan happily jumped out of bed when I reminded him where we were going. This was the second time Lachlan had been to the waterpark where the group would be held today and each week. The first time he had been to the waterpark and enjoyed the waterslides and beach.

Lachlan had been part of a surfing group previously two years before at a different beach in another location. The venue today had a small beach but I wondered whether Lachlan would be confused about attending the junior surfers group there in a new location with a different set of people, when he had previously entertained himself in a different way there.

There were lots of children, parents and group instructors all busy as they tried to find the right place to be. Parents and children looked for the right age groups and instructors to register with. Lachlan was a little disturbed by so many people being in one place at one time and he covered his ears to block out the loud noises from people talking.

When we found the right age group we saw most of the other children sitting in a line waiting for the activities to start. Lachlan and I went for a short walk to the beach and we returned closer to the starting time of the activities after I explained to the instructor that waiting in the line would be too overwhelming for Lachlan. The instructor understood and told me that a support person would assist Lachlan once they arrived.

While we walked at the beach a young man approached us and I assumed this was Lachlan's assistant for the day. We will call him Josh. Josh was a young man who had come from the other side of town as a volunteer to support Lachlan. While Lachlan walked along a wall around the edge of the water, Josh noticed Lachlan's excellent balance immediately.

Lachlan liked Josh and led him in various directions along the beach and into the sand. He led him into the water and they walked further out into the deeper end. I wondered whether Josh would have felt comfortable enough to direct Lachlan back, given that it was the first time they had met. I was not concerned about Lachlan's safety but curious about where they were headed. I decided to get into the water myself as they had gone too far away to have heard me if I had called out to them. Lachlan and Josh had walked past two teams of older surfers who looked as though they were doing relay exercises.

The water was very cold and I wondered if this was the reason for Lachlan's earlier reluctance to enter the water. When I finally caught up to them I noticed Lachlan was pointing out a giant water slide to Josh which he wanted to have a turn on. Lachlan knew that his best chance of having a turn on the slide would have been by asking Josh, but the slide had not even begun to operate for the day.

Every now and then I tried to draw Lachlan back to his group who were involved in various games and races but he found being around so many other children a little overwhelming. There were too many new faces all in the one place and it was too noisy for him. He happily walked around near the group and was interested in the games they played, but at this stage it seemed more natural for Lachlan to want to keep his distance.

Lachlan watched while the children's swimming and floating skills were being assessed. Part of him wanted to join in and show the other children that he also knew how to do those things. He would join in when he was ready. Lachlan was excited to collect his junior surfers' uniform at the end of the session. Lachlan had a ball. Thank you Josh!

Chapter 12
December 2015

Tuesday 01/12/15

This morning was a speech therapy consultation with Debbie regarding food issues. Since the last appointment Lachlan had gone back to eating his usual dinner as well as cheese on toast, gingerbread, and other biscuits and crackers. This was fantastic! We are working on apples and other types of cheese and between now and the next appointment we plan to try garlic bread, dark brown bread, oven baked rolls, dried noodles, bacon and muesli bars. Debbie also suggested to cut the bread in different ways and use different spreads and different crockery which should stop Lachlan from becoming tired of the same foods.

Thursday 03/12/15

This morning Itsal woke Lachlan as usual. Lachlan wanted to pat him and he sat on Lachlan's bed (which is Itsal's bed also), until he was instructed to prompt Lachlan to get out of bed. Itsal nudged Lachlan's legs and arms in the gaps not covered by his pyjamas. Itsal licked Lachlan's arm to remind him that the morning school routine needed to begin.

Itsal does not do this at any other time as he knows Lachlan may not like it. Itsal also knew that doing this would bring about the response we hoped for as Lachlan quickly rose from the bed and strangely enough was not annoyed at all. Lachlan understood what he needed to do and did it.

Itsal went to visit the vet this morning as he had urinated a few times inside the house which had not happened before. He was happy to go inside where he was weighed and examined and his temperature was taken. It seemed that Itsal had a urine infection and was given a course of antibiotics to take.

Itsal is the first dog I have been able to easily administer medication to. He trusted me and allowed me to do it. He did not seem bothered in the slightest by having the tablet placed in his throat. He did not try and move away or even budge from his sitting position which was unlike other dogs I had known before.

Today was Lachlan's end of year school concert. When his class came out for their performance, I looked for him but was unable to find him on stage for some time. Eventually I realised he had been there all along but as his hair had been styled for the performance, I had not recognised him! His hair had been teased and stuck out and he wore a black T-shirt covered in green glittery circles with black shorts and he had green tinsel tied to his wrists.

As the performance continued the children took turns and danced one at time at the front of the stage. When Lachlan had his turn he had a huge smile on his face. He did not seem shy at all, quite the opposite as he seemed to enjoy dancing and the attention he received from the crowd. He looked happy and comfortable, like a seasoned performer. What a huge relief to see him so at ease and happy in his school environment.

Sunday 06/12/15

Lachlan went to the junior surfers group for the second time this season. His assistant was a woman which we will call Kylie. Lachlan and Kylie went out into the surf until all I could see of them were two dots in the sea. They moved up and down in the waves and at times disappeared beneath the waves. Lachlan had the time of his life and as this beach had no rip currents to worry about, it was much safer in the water than usual. The depth of the water also allowed Lachlan to stand.

When the relays started Lachlan and Kylie ran up and down and joined in with the others in the team. Lachlan is a very fast runner but needed some inspiration to join in, as he much preferred to be in waves. Being extremely strong in his body Lachlan could easily have run the relay race quickly had he have been motivated to do so. However, he still participated and ran at his own pace.

Monday 07/12/15

Itsal woke me early this morning, he did not touch me but sat next to my bed which was enough to wake me. As Itsal is currently having treatment for a urine infection I assumed he must have needed the toilet. When I took him to the door, he did not want to go outside to the toilet. He also did not lead me to Lachlan's room so I knew there was nothing to be concerned about in there. As I wondered why Itsal had woken me, I checked the time and noticed that my alarm which should have sounded ten minutes before, had not worked. This made me realise that Itsal had woken me because the alarm had failed to work. Thanks Itsal!

This evening Lachlan touched my nose and signed the "More" sign. He did this a few times as I tried to work out what he was asking me. He laughed as he touched my nose which made me realise that he wanted to play the game whereby, I steal his nose. He thinks this game is hilarious even though he knows for a fact there is no nose in my fist. He has forced my fist open many times revealing a coloured painted fingernail, which did not matter as he still enjoyed the silliness of the game.

Tuesday 08/12/15

Itsal reminded me that it was time for his medication as he sat and nudged my hand towards his medication. It did not take very long for Itsal to realise that a routine had started and that he needed to have the tablets twice daily.

Wednesday 09/12/15

Today was Lachlan's last school day for the term which he was quite excited about. He wore his own clothes and wanted to wait outside in the street until the bus arrived. The bus driver gave him a box of chocolates as a gift, which he unwrapped and when he saw them signed "Finished" so that I would take them away. Lachlan eats only one type of chocolate and even that is rare.

Lachlan's end of year school report was very positive and they remarked that he was always joyous and happy and had made great progress with reading, spelling and communication.

In the afternoon Lachlan wanted to make peanut butter sandwiches which he had not eaten since he was in preschool! It is always very exciting when Lachlan goes back to eating a food or expands his interest in new foods. I had also placed some strawberries in his view hoping that he may go back to eating them again, but not this time.

Saturday 12/12/15

Samantha spent the evening with Lachlan and babysat. They went for a drive to look at local houses which were lit up with Christmas lights. One house had a huge display in its front window and Santa Claus was there, which made it Lachlan's favourite house.

Sunday 13/12/15

Lachlan woke early to get ready for the junior surfing group at the beach. Lachlan had a different assistant, a young man. Lachlan's first task was to learn about water safety in the pool. The pool was quite cold and Lachlan was a little reluctant to enter it however, when the other children came out of the pool, Lachlan wanted to go in as he preferred to swim by himself.

Later in the day Lachlan's nanna visited along with his big sister Samantha. Every now and then Lachlan gave his nanna a big bear hug. She did not seem to mind his roughness at all; in fact she was amused by it once again.

In the evening Lachlan went to carols by candlelight. There was a jumping castle which he liked and when he had to wait his turn because the older boys were having their turn, he found a place on the front corner of the castle where he could jump up and down a little while he waited.

As the evening became darker, fewer of the children noticed Itsal as he waited at the side of the jumping castle for Lachlan. Itsal always attracts a lot of attention but the children had been respectful and seemed to understand the 'no patting' rule. When the carols started we were amazed to see Lachlan sitting and enjoying them all. Itsal lay at his feet and at times, because he was so close, Lachlan gently kicked him. Lachlan followed the words of the carols from the booklet. He seemed to really enjoy the singing and music being played. This was another wonderful experience which would not have been possible without Itsal as Lachlan would have been overwhelmed by the people and noise.

Lachlan was very pleased as usual to see Karen who ran the carols night. Lachlan liked how Karen communicated with him as she used hand signs which meant Lachlan understood every part of their interaction. Karen has always taken the time to communicate effectively with Lachlan and the two of them have built a very positive relationship. Thank you Karen!

Monday 14/12/15

We needed to buy some groceries so I mentioned to Lachlan that soon we would go shopping. Five minutes later Lachlan called me to the computer and showed me a picture of a shop he had searched for online and made it clear that was where he wanted to go.

We did the grocery shopping and one of the workers who is always friendly towards Lachlan had noticed that he seemed a lot more settled. She was surprised when Lachlan loaded all the grocery items onto the counter and lifted the heavy bags easily into the trolley.

In the afternoon we visited the shop Lachlan had now requested twice. He had asked a second time by showing me a different photo of the shop which he had also found online. It was the same shop but at a different shopping centre which Lachlan had visited once previously.

When we arrived at the shopping centre I quickly took a mental note of the location and of where we had parked and I noted the first shop we had passed on the way into the shopping centre. Even though Lachlan had only visited this centre once before and long ago he found the shop immediately and checked out the DVDs as usual. Next he went on some rides and looked in a few other shops where he found the theme song for a children's movie he liked and played it until it was time to leave.

On our way out we came across the shop we first saw as we entered the car park (or so we thought), so we continued our walk to the car park. Mysteriously, nothing seemed familiar and the underground car park was now an open-air car park. Something was wrong as I knew I had not parked in the outdoor car park. I tried not to let Lachlan know we were lost as I didn't want to alarm him and I casually told him that we would find the car if we looked a little more. After a few minutes I asked Lachlan which way we should go and he pointed to a specific spot in the car park. I followed him until the car park looked familiar again. Lachlan suddenly pointed to a car we had almost passed and sure enough, there it was! The mystery was solved. There were two shops of the same kind on the same floor roughly one hundred meters apart. Thanks Lachlan!

Tuesday 15/12/15

Lachlan spent the morning playing in the backyard spa. While he was in there Itsal started barking rather fiercely which indicated someone was at the front door. Itsal and I went inside to investigate and Itsal barked again at the front door. As I went to open the door, Itsal latched onto my wrist with his mouth and led me away from the door. After I gave Itsal a command he released my wrist from his grip. Just as I was about to open the door again, Itsal jumped up and pushed me away from the door. The way he acted made me wonder who or what was outside.

After I waited a few minutes I opened the door and at the same moment I saw a car speed off down the street. Itsal will sometimes bark at people visiting one of the houses in our street. It is usually the same house so I figured there must have been an altercation of some kind there or perhaps a visitor he did not like.

Wednesday 16/12/15

Itsal woke me around 5.30 a.m. by nudging my arm. I think I fell back to sleep and Itsal left and came back a few minutes later and tried to wake me once more. Lachlan was awake and moving about in his room and Itsal had wanted me to know that Lachlan was awake and unsupervised.

Lachlan began pulling out the drawers as though he was on a mission to find something. Eventually he found what he was looking for which was one of his father's old aeroplane magazines. Lachlan studied each of the planes in the magazine which took an hour or more. He flicked the pages back and forth and compared the different aeroplanes.

After breakfast we visited Lachlan's aunt's house where he had a swim in the pool. It was quite a cold day for summer but not cold enough to deter Lachlan from swimming. He swam for three hours by himself before he signed "Finished". While Lachlan swam in the pool Itsal had a break from duty and played with Lulu, Lachlan's aunt's new puppy. Lulu barked excitedly at Lachlan when he first arrived a few times trying to request his attention. Lachlan was a little frightened as Lulu went near his feet and he was not able to control her rapid puppy movements. Lachlan's aunt came to the rescue as she put Lulu's lead on which prevented her from getting too close to Lachlan.

While Itsal and Lulu played, Itsal held two of Lulu's toys in his mouth not wanting to share them with her. Both dogs were excited and chased each other constantly and when Itsal returned home he was tired and sleepy.

This evening Lachlan went to look at local houses which had been decorated with Christmas lights. On the drive Lachlan pointed out and appreciated each and every house which was decorated with coloured lights even the ones with just a few lights. Lachlan would have happily looked at lights on houses for hours but settled for one hour.

Thursday 17/12/15

Lachlan spent most of the day in the backyard spa even though the water was not warm. In the afternoon Danielle came to our house to give Lachlan a haircut. Before her arrival I had shown Lachlan the visuals which represented this so he was prepared and happy when she arrived. He moved outside on the verandah, the usual spot for haircuts. We chatted to Danielle as usual about all sorts of things while she cut Lachlan's hair and Lachlan listened to our conversation. Itsal sat next to Lachlan who held onto Itsal's neck at times. Lachlan was very relaxed while he had his haircut today. Towards the end of the haircut Lachlan signed "Finished" and we began a countdown from twenty to one which allowed Danielle enough time to quickly finish the haircut while acknowledging Lachlan's request to end the haircut. Straight after the haircut Lachlan ran to open his present which Danielle had bought him, a train, which Lachlan was very excited about.

Friday 18/12/15

Sometimes when Lachlan returns to a place he has not been to for a long time it highlights how he has changed physically and developmentally. We went back to a pool which we visited one year ago and it was amazing to see how well he handled the wave pool without hands on support and that without any further organised swimming lessons his water confidence and swimming skills had advanced. We went into the Olympic pool and I noticed Lachlan was able to swim well on his back by kicking and having his arms out to the side. Another change I noticed was that Lachlan was much more careful around other children and gave them the room they needed which was something he was unaware of a year ago.

Sunday 20/12/15

There was a visit from Santa at the end of the junior surfers group today. Santa was handing out lollies to the children. Lachlan was interested, so went to see Santa and he watched the other children as they received lollies from him. Next Santa offered Lachlan a lolly which was wrapped in plastic. Lachlan took it but looked into Santa's lolly bag to see if there was anything he may have liked more. When Lachlan saw that all the lollies were the same type he put the one Santa had just given him back into Santa's bag with the others! Santa laughed and then offered one to me. I accepted it to be polite but probably would not have eaten it. Lachlan did not see the need to be polite.

Lachlan watched a cartoon in Spanish and eventually wanted to change it back to English. Knowing that he needed our help to change it back to English he thought of a way to ask for help. He found the words 'English Subtitles' on the back of a DVD cover in his collection and pointed those words out. Then he pointed to the computer and we knew exactly what he wanted.

I really think he remembers each word on all of the DVDs and the cases, as he often uses them to communicate something to us.

In the afternoon we went to post some parcels, six to be exact. Lachlan likes to help with this but today when we arrived at the post box it was full, so Lachlan could only place one of the parcels inside the post box. Lachlan became a little distressed as he likes to finish things and he knew all the parcels needed to be posted.

While I explained to him that we would go to the post office nearby to post the rest of the parcels, a man approached us from one of the neighbouring houses having heard Lachlan calling out. He was holding a small long haired black dog. The man asked if everything was alright and I told him that it was, that the post box was full and that we just needed to find another one. Next the man asked me if Lachlan would like to play with his dog, hoping it might cheer him up. I told the man that Lachlan was not very keen on dogs he was unfamiliar with and thanked him, but declined the offer on Lachlan's behalf.

Next the man asked whether I liked dogs and told us about how friendly his dog was. The man asked whether I wanted to pat his dog which I did in order to show Lachlan that I was not afraid. Lachlan seemed pleased but was not interested in patting the dog himself.

Christmas Eve 24/12/15

When Lachlan was playing on the computer this morning he called me over to show me a photo of a shop he was interested in going to. Lachlan showed me a photo of a shop in Cairns (interstate) but knew the same shop was also at one of the local shopping centres which he hoped I would take him to today. I was not keen on going to that particular shopping centre as I knew Lachlan would not have liked the crowds on Christmas Eve. I showed Lachlan my grocery list and asked if he could help with this and he nodded in agreement.

A short while later Lachlan called me back to the computer where he had found two DVDs he wanted to buy in an online shop. One of them sounded familiar and I thought he already had it in his collection. When I asked him if he did he shook his head, but I was not convinced so I looked through the whole collection which was over three hundred of them and found he was right, the one he wanted was not there.

Next Lachlan handed me my shopping list and pointed again to the names of two DVDs he had found online, then he pointed to my shopping list. I knew he wanted me to write the names of the DVDs on the list which I did as I tried to think of a way to explain that these DVDs would not be available at the grocery shop we were headed to.

Then I remembered about Santa and I pretended to ring him on behalf of Lachlan and ask for the two DVDs for Christmas. Lachlan nodded the whole time to show he fully approved of this idea.

Christmas Day! 25/12/15

Lachlan woke at the usual time and I reminded him that it was Christmas Day, not that most children would need reminding about that, but I reminded him anyway. He watched his DVD as usual and I asked him to look near the Christmas tree as Santa had been to visit.

Nanna had stayed at our house on Christmas Eve, so Lachlan gave her a hug on the way to the Christmas tree. Lachlan was excited when he saw all the presents and insisted he open Itsal's gifts first which we had wrapped together previously. Lachlan knew what was inside with those presents and wanted no surprises when he began opening the presents.

Lachlan studied the presents and tried to find ones which looked like they may have contained a DVD. Once he found the DVDs he had hoped for he watched them and did not open any other presents for some time. He would have been happy with the DVDs alone and eventually he opened the rest of the presents throughout the day. His two favourites were some train DVDs and some water balloons.

Later on at the family Christmas lunch, Uncle Jim gave Lachlan a football jersey and some shorts and Lachlan wanted to wear them straight away so he changed into them. I had never seen him quite so interested in clothes before, except for swimming gear (which would indicate a swim was not far away).

Lachlan loved seeing his uncles and cousins which are all boys, and I noticed he approached each of them at different times and asked to be picked up by those he knew were strong enough to do so. He wanted to play rough with them and they all happily went along with it.

At one stage Lachlan ran into the vacant newly built house next door. Itsal was quick to notice and chased after him even though he was not in working mode and did not have his jacket on. Lachlan just wanted to walk along the wall as he often did and was in no harm. He would need to stop visiting the new house once the new neighbours moved in.

Lachlan did not eat any of the Christmas food just his bread rolls as usual. Later in the afternoon he played on his new water slide which was a Christmas present and went to bed very tired and happy and fell asleep easily as I did on the bean bag next to his bed.

Saturday 26/12/15

Today was a great day for the beach but to avoid sunburn and being in the water at the hottest time of the day we went to an equestrian centre nearby until the cooler part of the day came. Lachlan loves horses and he watched them carefully in their stalls and some as they were being walked around the yard. He seemed to like the graceful way they moved much the same way as he enjoys watching birds flying. He notices things like that.

Lachlan can never have too much of the beach. He liked the wild surf at the beach we had chosen and we were able to park close by. Some rip currents were present and the swimming flags were close together. Every ten minutes or so we found ourselves almost outside the flags and had to get out and make our way back to the safe area between the two flags. I explained to Lachlan a few times why this was important and tried to point out the currents beyond the flags which indicated unsafe areas of the beach. After the second time I had said, "Back to the flags," Lachlan dutifully got out of the water and ran back to the flags, taking me literally.

At times we forget that he will make the most literal interpretation of our words and I chose my words more carefully after that. Lachlan is also keen on boats of all kinds and was interested at seeing the Sydney to Hobart race headed down the coast some distance out to sea. However, after an hour the weather started to appear overcast and looked like rain so I did an abbreviated version of the countdown we often use to mark the end of enjoyable things; swimming, to a less enjoyable thing; going home. As it turned out, by the time we were changed and back at the car the weather had cleared, but we left anyway as Lachlan now expected this.

Lachlan ate a chocolate Santa today. That may not be unusual for other children but for him it is like a small miracle when he tries a new food. Exactly as Debbie had told us, Lachlan first touched the chocolate on his cheek, then his lips as it came closer to his mouth before he tasted it. He held it in his hand for a while scratching his nail up and down its surface while it melted in his hand as he ate tiny pieces every now and then.

Tuesday 29/12/15

This morning at breakfast time Itsal stood near the laundry basket and nudged it with his nose. He kept on nudging it and moved it to the back door. He was letting me know that the basket should be outside and yes, he was right, so I opened the door and put the basket in the

346

laundry and Itsal took this opportunity to go outside to the toilet. What an unusual way to ask to go outside, I thought.

Today Lachlan helped bake some chocolate chip muffins which we hoped would spark his interest to try them. Lachlan currently eats chocolate chip muffins but they must be bought from a particular shop, and yes he can definitely tell the difference. Debbie had suggested that if Lachlan assisted with cooking it may help him become less sensitive to foods, and you never know he just might try one. Lachlan was happy to place the dry ingredients – flour, sugar and chocolate chips into a bowl and mix them. When I added a bowl of wet ingredients-egg and milk, Lachlan gagged as he found seeing the sticky mess very unpleasant. He continued with the mixing even though it had made him feel physically sick and I needed to tell him that I would do it and he did not need to help. Lachlan was interested in the muffins once they were cooked and even picked one up but did not eat it. That was a good start.

Thursday 31/12/15

Once it became dark, we went to look at a house with beautiful Christmas displays and lights. Lachlan would have been too tired to attend any new year celebrations later in the evening as he had woken twice the night before and had stayed awake for long periods as he had been a little unwell.

The house we visited had the most spectacular Christmas display and people had come from all over to see it. Lachlan ruffled the beard of the life size Santa mannequin. He wanted to check whether or not it was real like the ones he had seen in shopping centres. He looked at the window display for some time and watched the miniature trains go around on their tracks. There was a cuckoo clock which had a little snowman that popped out of the windows every now and then which Lachlan was amused by. The paths were lit up with coloured lights and there were all kinds of animals displayed in lights. There was also a collection of soft toys and Lachlan was amazed when he saw how many there were although he did not want to stay very long. He was tired and wanted to go home. On the way home I drove to a location on a hill where people often stood and watched the local firework displays. We were able to see some of the firework display, enough to keep Lachlan happy until he signed "Finish" and we went home to sleep.

This year has been Lachlan's best year yet. He has been happy to go to school every day during the year (with the exception of three days). He achieved two of his goals by learning to surf on the simulator and by participating in a junior surfing group at the beach. Lachlan was thrilled to receive a certificate and ribbon from the surfing group for his participation in the program and events.

We are very grateful for the grant and support Lachlan received from My Choice Matters to run this project and follow his dream. We are also very grateful to the swim centre and Lachlan's fantastic surf instructor and for the support Lachlan received from the surfing group who provided a dedicated volunteer most weeks to assist. This has been Lachlan's best summer so far.

Itsal has been a wonderful influence and having him as part of the family has given Lachlan more confidence that we could have ever thought possible. We had no idea of just how many changes we would see and we are forever grateful to Joanne Baker and the team at Righteous Pups Australia for working so hard to make a difference not only to Lachlan but the whole family.

Lachlan's speech has improved and Itsal has assisted him to enter shopping centres in a calm manner, without feeling the need to abscond. He alerts us at night so that Lachlan is never left unsupervised and he provides companionship and has had a positive influence on Lachlan's peer relationships. Itsal has taught Lachlan to be responsible by caring for him especially with the daily feeding routine, and he has helped with desensitizing Lachlan to some foods which he handles for Itsal's benefit.

Lachlan will now wait in turn in queues and ride in elevators. He is now able to travel for extended periods and is happier to sit for longer lengths of time. He is assisted during haircuts. Itsal has allowed us to take the path of least resistance.

Lachlan is less concerned about sensitivities which allows him to enjoy activities further and concentrate on forming relationships with other people while he is less self-absorbed and more focussed.

Thanks to Debbie Alvarez, Lachlan's diet has expanded and we have seen some fantastic changes and thanks to Lachlan whenever I go out and see someone eating unusual looking food, instead of wondering about the reason why, I wonder if it is a minor miracle that the person is eating that food. Thanks for opening our eyes Lachlan.

We are grateful to our family and friends for inviting us to gatherings even though we often need to leave early to keep Lachlan within his established routine. We know you understand and hope that when we have to race off mid-sentence during a conversation to check on Lachlan, you will still think it is worth trying to have another conversation at some point. Any opportunity for Lachlan to get together with family and friends and new activities can involve a lot of trial and error.

Activities for Lachlan seem to be a balance between trying to fit in within mainstream activities and joining up with other children with special needs where sometimes the expectations can be very low. It is ideal for Lachlan to be supported within a mainstream setting and to be involved in the same activities as other children his age. As parents we would never want to tell him he is too disabled to achieve his goals. We would not want to limit him in this way. After all, no one really knows what another person is capable of doing. We are continually surprised by Lachlan's capabilities.